CONTENTS

FOREWORD

The greatness of a nation and its moral progress can be judged by the way its animals are treated.
Mahatma Gandhi

According to a survey conducted by the Romanian Ministry of Tourism in Great Britain in 2006, the magic words that lure British people to Romania are 'unspoiled nature'. And after working for many years as a wildlife guide in the Romanian Carpathians and the Danube Delta I can definitely say that eastern and central Europe has this in abundance. Gerard Gorman remarks that the countries of the region 'have many things in common, not in the least the fact that until the early 1990s very few visitors from the West were willing or able to explore them'. What an encouraging sign, then, that these visitors started discovering and exploring these countries first of all for their wilderness.

What is perhaps most fascinating is that many of these countries have managed to preserve their amazingly rich wildlife alongside their traditional farming practices. This means that any wildlife-watching trip also becomes a way of discovering the region's traditional culture. The big challenge now is to preserve this rich natural environment for future generations. A very sensible approach to wildlife management is needed, with a key factor being an awareness that protecting wildlife represents a benefit both for nature itself and for the people living in or close to the protected areas.

Books like this are taking important steps towards this awareness, by addressing every person with an interest in wildlife. It is encouraging that the writer not only has great experience with wildlife and conservation, but has also lived a good part of his life through the dramatic changes in this part of Europe.

Bradt have come up with a great initiative: an invitation to discover the natural treasures of this complex historical region. I hope that, by travelling to any of the places mentioned in this book, you will experience for yourself the healthy and natural way in which people can still live together with the wildlife around them.

Dan Marin, wildlife guide
Joint winner of the Paul Morrison Wanderlust Tour Guide Award 2007

Bellowing red deer stag (DT)

ABOUT THE AUTHOR

Gerard Gorman was born in England but has lived on the continent since the 1980s, mostly in Hungary. He has travelled extensively in the countries of central and eastern Europe, mostly when in search of wildlife. His previous books include *The Birds of Hungary* (Christopher Helm), *Woodpeckers of Europe* (Bruce Coleman) and *Birding in Eastern Europe* (Wildsounds). In 1995 he was awarded the first Eric Hoskings Trust Writing Bursary for a project entitled 'Birds and Political Change in Eastern Europe'. When not watching or writing about the wildlife, he runs a guiding service (*www.probirder.com*) for visiting birders, lepidopterists and other naturalists. To date, he has led over 400 group tours in the region.

ACKNOWLEDGEMENTS

I am indebted to many friends who accompanied me in the field, particularly Josef Chytil, Gabor Kovacs, Samuel Pacenovsky, Eugen Petrescu and Andras Schmidt. Many others have supplied me with notes on the wildlife and wild places of their respective countries; they include Uku Paal, Mati Kose (Estonia), Agris Celmens, Valdis Pilats (Latvia), Juozas Miskinis (Lithuania), Waldemar Krasowski, Felix Felger (Poland), Sandor Boldogh (Hungary), Zoltan Baczo, Daniel Petrescu (Romania), Dimiter Georgiev, Nicky Petkov, Milen Marinov (Bulgaria), Andrej Bibic (Slovenia), Gordon Lukacs, Jelena Kralj (Croatia), Milan Paunovic, Dragan Simic (Serbia) and Peter Mackelworth (marine wildlife). Chris Durdin and Kester Eddy kindly commented on sections of the text. Special thanks to Mary Stevenson who corrected an early draft and made many important corrections. I am also very grateful to Tricia Hayne, Mike Miles, Adrian Phillips, Marianne Taylor, Mike Unwin and all the staff at Bradt for taking this title on board and bringing it to fruition.

The magnificent caves at
Aggtelek, Hungary (FB)

CENTRAL & EASTERN EUROPE

EUROPE

N
Bradt

Narva
TALLINN
Hiiumaa
Lake Peipsi
Saaremaa
ESTONIA

RUSSIAN FEDERATION

Gulf of Riga
LATVIA
RIGA
BALTIC SEA
Liepāja
Daugova
Daugavpils
Klaipéda
LITHUANIA
KALININGRAD
Gulf of Gdansk
Neman
Kaunas
RUSSIA
VILNIUS
Gdansk
Elblag
Szczecin
Bialystok
BELARUS
Bydgoszcz
POLAND
0   300km
0   200 miles
Poznań
Warta
WARSAW
Bug
Odra
GERMANY
Wrocław
Łódź
Lublin
Opope
Wisła
San
PRAGUE
Kraków
UKRAINE
CZECH
Sudeten
Plzeň
REPUBLIC
Vltava
Ostrava
2655m
SLOVAKIA
Košice
Miskolc
MOLDOVA
BRATISLAVA
Danube
Prut
Suceava
Iasi
AUSTRIA
Debrecen
Carpathians
BUDAPEST
Tisza
Siret
HUNGARY
Clujnapoca
Maribor
Arad
Mures
SLOVENIA
ZAGREB
Subotica
ROMANIA
LJUBLJANA
Dráva
Timisoara
ITALY
Rijeka
Sava
Novi Sad
2544m
Brasov
Golf di
CROATIA
Danube
BELGRADE
Venézia
Transylvanian Alps
BUCHAREST
Lošinj
BOSNIA &
Olt
Zadar
HERZEGOVINA
SERBIA
Ruse
Constanta
Dugi Otok
SARAJEVO
2522m
Danube
BLACK
Split
Morava
SEA
Brač
Dubrovnik
Niš
BULGARIA
Varna
Korčula
Prištir
SOFIA
Balkans
MONTENEGRO
KOSOVO/A
PODGORICA
Plovdiv
TURKEY
2925m
ADRIATIC
ALBANIA
MACE-
SEA
DONIA
GREECE
AEGEON
SEA

KEY
Capital
Town
Airport (international)
Mountain peak
Land over 3000m

INTRODUCTION

This guide covers a selection of the wildlife of central and eastern Europe. This region is here defined as 15 countries from the Baltic Sea in the north to the Adriatic and Black seas in the south: Bosnia & Herzegovina, Bulgaria, Croatia, Czech Republic, Estonia, Hungary, Kaliningrad Oblast, Latvia, Lithuania, Montenegro, Poland, Romania, Serbia, Slovakia and Slovenia. These countries are all different, but they also have many things in common, not least the fact that until the early 1990s very few visitors from the West were willing or able to explore them. They are

Brown bear: emblematic of the wild places of central and eastern Europe (Jiří Bohdal/Naturfoto)

also similar in that they are remarkably rich in wildlife, home to species that are scarce, or which have vanished entirely, from countries further west. One of the aims of this book is to introduce that wildlife. Excellent field guides are available to help you identify the species you may encounter and this book does not aim to compete with these; rather it aims to provide an overview of, and insights into, the region's wildlife. Getting to the countries included has never been easier: today, there are plenty of low-cost airlines, no visas are required and there is a good selection of practical travel guides (including Bradt's own series) to help you on the ground once you arrive. Thus general tourist and travelling information has been kept to a minimum in this book.

TAXONOMY: WHAT'S IN A NAME?

Each major taxonomic group is given a separate chapter (Mammals, Birds, Reptiles, Amphibians, Invertebrates) covered in this book. However, a book of this size cannot possibly cover everything, thus some species (usually those that are widespread in the west of Europe) are excluded, with the focus on those of a more eastern distribution. Of the invertebrates, only butterflies and dragonflies are covered in detail, as they are the two orders that are most likely to be seen by the traveller and to which comprehensive field guides are available – to adequately cover other insect orders would have taken a much longer book.

I have taken the liberty of being flexible with taxonomic order. For example, in the chapter on birds, species from quite different families are mentioned side by side under headings which reflect habitats; for example, the great bustard, larks and wheatears are treated together in the section on grassland birds. Taxonomic nomenclature is a controversial field; often several English vernacular names are available for the same species, and there is little agreement between the various 'authorities' on international usage. I have bypassed this debate and generally used those names found in the standard field guides (see *Further Information*). Where in doubt, scientific names should be referred to, as these rarely vary. For example, in this book *Aegypius monachus* is called the black vulture, but this bird is also known as the Eurasian black vulture, monk vulture and cinereous vulture – thankfully the scientific name is always the same. The name of a species is always in two parts and in italics (an italicised binomial). The first word indicates the genus, the second the exact species. Subspecies, or races, are indicated by the use of a three-part name (trinomial). The following simple example illustrates how taxonomic terminology works:

Wolf

Kingdom	Animalia (animals)
Phylum	Chordata (chordates – animals with spinal cords)
Class	Mammalia (mammals)
Order	Carnivora (carnivores – meat-eaters)
Family	Canidae (dogs)
Genus	*Canis* (dog)
Species	*Canis lupus* (wolf)
Subspecies	*Canis lupus lupus* (Eurasian or grey wolf),
	Canis lupus italicus (Italian wolf)

LANDSCAPES AND HABITATS

The Julian Alps in Slovenia (TT)

The word 'habitat' can be used to describe a general area, such as a forest or a wetland, or an exact location, such as that of a single plant or the soil beneath a log. The former might be called a landscape, or more correctly a biome. Biomes are named after their main vegetation or landscape feature, such as grassland or wetland, but are actually complex patchworks of habitats. Whatever its size, a habitat provides the resources, such as food and shelter, to sustain an organism or organisms. In this book the word habitat is used in its most simple form, to mean a place or environment where an animal lives.

Different animals require different habitats and these habitats may be shared – by different species, by similar species or by several members of the same species. Most animals use a variety of habitats depending on the stages of their life, season and even the time of day. Some live in very specific habitats when at the edge of their range, but are less choosy at the heart of that range. Animals have evolved to live in and utilise their habitats. When a species is removed, its habitat will usually remain, but when habitat is destroyed, very few species can survive. For the naturalist, a knowledge of a particular animal's habitat goes hand in hand with a knowledge of the animal itself. Central and eastern Europe is a veritable mosaic of biomes and habitats; some of the most important are described below.

CLIMATE

Habitat is heavily linked to climate. Much depends upon latitude, altitude and geography, but most of the region is typically continental, with warm, dry summers and cold, snowy winters. Four seasons are discernible, though the distinction is often blurred. Local climates in the Baltic States, Croatia and other Balkan countries are subject to maritime influences, while landlocked countries like Hungary, Serbia, the Czech Republic and Slovakia are less so and thus see lower winter temperatures. Most countries experience extremes in temperature: from below zero in winter, to 35°C or more in summer.

THE LIE OF THE LAND

There is great variation in the land relief of the region, and even within individual countries. Overall, the south is more mountainous (especially in the Balkans) and the north typified by lowlands (part of the East European Plain). A significant feature is the Carpathian Basin, a flat lowland that is encircled by the Carpathians and the Alps and cut through by the Danube. The region's rivers belong to two main drainage basins – the Elbe in the north and the Danube in the south. The Czech Republic and Slovakia sit on the watershed between these two systems. Water from the springs and snow-melt of some of Europe's most impressive mountain ranges – Julian Alps, Dinaric Alps, Carpathians, Balkan Range – mostly ends up in the Adriatic, Baltic or Black seas and ultimately the North Sea and the Mediterranean.

FOREST AND WOODLAND

The word 'forest' describes a large area of dense tree cover with a closed canopy, while 'woodland' covers a smaller area and is fairly open. Forests and woodlands are very complex, both in terms of their structure and the variety of species found in them. Their biodiversity is high. Tree composition is influenced by factors such as latitude, elevation, precipitation and soil type. Some of the richest woodlands, in the heart of the continent, are deciduous, with mixed tree species such as lime, oak, elm, hornbeam and beech. Most of the region's large animals, such as European bison, red deer, brown bear and wolf, do well in such woodlands.

In the colder and wetter north there is more coniferous cover with spruce, fir, pine and larch often dominating. The taiga belt, open forest typified by pine, larch, birch and aspen, reaches into the Baltic states. Typical mammals here are elk, beavers, pine martens and lynxes. Lowlands and coastal areas, in the drier south, are covered by so-called Mediterranean woodlands. Typical trees here include various oaks, pines, chestnut and also areas of wild and cultivated olive trees. Much of Europe was once heavily forested but by the Middle Ages most of the old-growth had been felled. Since then humankind has greatly influenced and shaped the continent's wooded places with the economic activity of forestry. Modern forestry practices leave little scope for natural forest regeneration; however, some stands of old-growth remain in the east.

MOUNTAINS

Mountains are often the only truly wild areas in a country, but they have remained so by accident rather than by design. By their very nature mountains are difficult to access and the land is often less fertile than in lowlands. No surprise then, that

Snow-covered peaks in the Julian Alps, Slovenia (AB)

humankind has often left these places to themselves and, in the face of the march of 'civilisation', large carnivores such as brown bear and wolf retreated into mountains and established their last refuges there. Having said that, there are winter sport complexes in most of the higher ranges in central and eastern Europe and in Bulgaria, for example, ski-resort and building developments are surging ahead at a worrying pace.

At the highest elevations, above the treeline, mountain terrain can be harsh, typified by tundra, boulder fields, scree, rock walls, ravines, isolated tarns, moors and subarctic peatbogs. Much of this is blanketed in snow for long spells of the year. Yet these habitats sustain a diverse range of species – chamois, Alpine marmot, wallcreeper, Alpine salamander and Alpine newt – which have evolved to do well here. Montane meadows are key places for butterflies, many of which have very precise and subtle habitat requirements. Bosnia-Herzegovina, Bulgaria, Montenegro, Romania, Serbia, Slovakia and Slovenia are the most mountainous countries in the region, with some truly impressive and often very rugged ranges. These are the best countries to visit to explore montane habitats.

GRASSLAND

Grassland is another versatile word that simply means an area where the dominant vegetation is grass of some kind. There are many types of grassland, in upland and lowlands. Some are dry (steppe), others lush or wet (pastures and meadows). They may be natural, or man-maintained (mown or grazed by livestock). Grassland is one of the most degraded and threatened habitats. Throughout the ages grasslands

Montane grasslands in Slovakia (FB)

have been ploughed up, cultivated and built upon. Formally large areas are now fragmented and remnants are often only found on steep slopes or where there are poor soils. Yet some extensive tracts remain in central and eastern Europe, particularly in the Carpathian Basin. These are home to burrowing mammals such as souslik and hamsters, and therefore also their predators, such as polecats and golden jackals. A great variety of birds, including bustards, larks, pipits and wheatears, use grasslands and they are also the most important habitats for butterflies.

In Hungary flat, lowland, grazing land is known as *puszta*. The largest expanses of this steppe-like habitat lie east of the Danube in the Hortobágy and Kiskunság areas. *Puszta* sometimes seems to be a barren and monotonous landscape, but there are subtle differences in its make-up according to soil type (and hence vegetation), rainfall and land use. Birds of prey do well here. Saker falcons, for example, can often be seen hunting burrowing mammals on the *puszta*. Another important grassland region is the rolling, lowland steppe of Dobrudja in eastern Romania and Bulgaria, one of the driest areas in Europe.

Upland karst marsh in Bulgaria (NP)

WETLANDS

The word 'wetland' also embraces a great variety of habitats. Lakes, lagoons, ponds, tarns, oxbows, marshes, bogs, mires and fens are all wetlands. The dominant element is, of course, water. Wetlands support a great range and density of wildlife, but exactly which species occur in any given wetland depends upon many factors. Wetlands are found at all elevations, from lagoons at sealevel to bogs above the treeline. They come in all shapes and sizes, from vast lakes to small pools, and can be deep or shallow, permanent or temporary.

Wild animals use wetlands in a myriad ways. There are truly aquatic species and species of wetland edges and margins. Some species spend all their lives there, others visit for one particular purpose, such as to breed, or simply to drink. Some species require open water, whilst others need vegetation, and many need both. As an example, some dragonflies are only found by flowing water, such as rivers, whilst others only live by still waters such as ponds. A great range of species from all orders also inhabit and exploit the ecotones where water meets land. Some of these, such as amphibians and dragonflies, have evolved to utilise both worlds.

Water chemistry is important to all wetland wildlife but to frogs, toads, newts and dragonflies it is crucial. It can mean the difference between a pond or bog being

Manmade fishpond systems often provide good habitats for wildlife. (KP)

alive with one species, hosting many species, or having none. Perhaps more than any other habitat, wetlands have been heavily exploited, degraded and influenced by humankind. Yet manmade wetlands such as fishpond systems, gravel pits and reservoirs can be good wildlife habitats. Many adaptable species, whose habitat requirements are not too exacting, use such artificial wetlands to feed, breed and shelter. All in all, wetlands, whether natural or artificial, are often the most productive places to search for and observe wildlife.

In the north of the region, from the Czech Republic to the Baltic States, there are many nutrient-rich bogs, mires, fens and marshes. Rather acidic upland bogs covered in sphagnum moss are typical. In the Carpathian Basin, especially in Hungary, there are shallow alkaline lakes and temporary saline marshes which evaporate in summer. Along the Black Sea coast there are large freshwater and brackish lagoons. The Danube Delta in Romania is a phenomenal wetland wildlife paradise: a maze of open and lily-clad lakes, marshes, backwaters and dense reedbeds, all interlinked by a network of channels.

RIVERINE HABITATS

Across most of Europe, natural riverine landscapes have been altered almost beyond recognition. Rivers have been largely regulated, alluvial floodplains drained, riparian forests felled and ground waters tampered with. The best-preserved and longest stretches of riverine habitat are found in central and eastern Europe.

A superb example is at Soutok, in the very southeast of the Czech Republic. Here, the Morava and Dyje rivers converge in a complex of natural floodplain forests, meadows, streams and oxbows. Fine mature oaks stand proud on drier areas while willows and poplars grow in boggy terrain. In spring the area floods, in summer the waters recede. Beavers are in their element here and the ponds and marshes are important spawning grounds for amphibians. The Morava and the Dyje are part of the Danube catchment area and that mighty river itself also has stretches of native woodland, in Slovakia, Hungary, Croatia, Serbia, Bulgaria and Romania, though plantations are the norm for much of its course.

THE COAST

Coastal saltwater habitats can be grouped into four basic types: estuaries with mud flats, sandy shores, rocky shores and open water. A great range of species inhabits these biomes, with the largest variety found in rocky habitats. Most are, however, minute creatures and fall beyond the scope of this book. Birds are often more conspicuous: a variety of shorebirds have evolved to feed on a range of shoreline habitats, some probe into sand, others pick food from tide-line debris or from rocks. Estuaries are complex places where rivers meet the sea. At high tide saline seawater

The windswept Baltic coast near the river Vistula, Poland (FB)

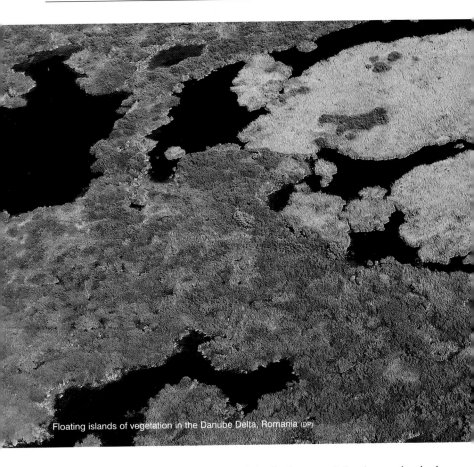

Floating islands of vegetation in the Danube Delta, Romania (DP)

heads up river, at low tide it retreats and the fresh water of the river pushes back. Very few animals are able to live in this fluctuating habitat mosaic permanently; most utilise estuaries only at certain times.

The Adriatic and Black seas are not very tidal, the sea only rising and falling by around 50cm, and shorelines are often rather narrow. The mainland coast of the Adriatic, from Slovenia to Montenegro, is more than 2,000km long and mostly rocky, dotted with saltpans and Mediterranean scrub. The Black Sea coast from the Danube Delta to the Bulgarian–Turkish border is around 580km long and, habitat-wise, very varied, with miles of saltmarshes, brackish lagoons and beaches. In both countries many sandy beaches are now tourist resorts, though some undeveloped stretches remain. In Romania, *grindul* are large sandy spits that, due to their inaccessibility and instability, are often wildlife refuges. Further south in Bulgaria there are more rocky, grassland-topped, headlands. The Baltic coastline from Poland to Estonia is over 5,000km long (including island shorelines) and is more tidal, with generally wider shorelines. One of the unique habitats here is the shifting dunes of the Curonian Spit in Kaliningrad and Lithuania.

ISLANDS

Islands are isolated biomes with habitats that are often in a more natural, less disturbed, state than similar habitats on the mainland. Though times have changed, their historic isolation and inaccessibility has often meant less interference from humankind. A lack of contact with mainland populations results in some sedentary species, particularly reptiles, evolving distinct local patterns and colorations; these local forms may in time become distinct island subspecies.

Islands are used by wildlife because they are places of refuge. Being isolated and surrounded by water, they are often good, safe places to rest or breed, as most land predators are unable or unwilling to swim across open water, especially the sea, and often suffer less human disturbance. In the Baltic, grey seals rarely come onto the mainland but habitually haul themselves up onto island shores. Many shorebirds and seabirds also establish breeding colonies on the safer offshore islands.

Estonia has more than 1,500 islands and islets, the largest of which are Saaremaa (2,673km²) and Hiiumaa (989km²). Many of the smaller islands are treeless and rather barren. Conservationists in Estonia are using the natural isolation of

Hiiumaa to good effect in the battle against the American mink. This alien species has driven European mink from most of its mainland habitats but it has failed to take over the island, which remains the realm of the native species, and an ongoing project aims to keep it that way.

Croatia's archipelago comprises more than 1,000 islands, which range in size from Krk (400km²) to small rocky islets off Lastovo and Mljet where Audouin's gulls breed. Just 66 Croatian islands have permanent settlements and, not surprisingly, the various habitats on the others have become wildlife havens.

THE HUMAN LANDSCAPE

As elsewhere on the planet, evidence of the hand of man is everywhere in central and eastern Europe. Though the region has some of the largest and best-preserved tracts of wetland, woodland and grassland on the continent, the signs of human influence on the landscape and the habitats within it are inescapable. But wildlife can be tenacious and some species have adapted to change. Much arable farmland is far from ideal wildlife habitat, but where it is not worked too intensively, and pesticide use is limited, birds in particular often do well. For example, in Hungary great bustards are more likely to be found in fields of lucerne and rape than on the grassy *puszta*. Deer, too, come out of their woodland homes to graze among crops. And just where did all those white storks nest before the invention of the telegraph pole, and where did rollers and shrikes perch before roadside telephone wires existed? Many bats use buildings as roosts and nurseries, to such an extent that they are often referred to as a distinct group, the 'house-dwelling bats'.

Commercial fishfarms are a familiar feature of lowland areas throughout the region. Some are hundreds of years old and in a semi-natural state, set amongst grasslands or forests and with thick reedbeds. Such fishponds are often the best wetland habitats locally. Though old-growth forests have a higher biodiversity than managed forests, and are the natural homes of many arboreal species, wildlife is sometimes easier to find and observe in 'artificial' habitat. As with farmland and fishponds, management is the key. Monocultures of fast growing same-age alien tree varieties will be largely devoid of wildlife. However, landscaped parks and arboretums can be good places to see red squirrels and woodland birds, which are often more confiding in such settings than in woodlands proper. The best parkland for wildlife is that planted with plenty of native tree species rather than exotic ones.

Geoffroy's bats often roost in buildings rather than in 'natural' sites. (PM)

MAMMALS

The steely gaze of a
European lynx (Bildagentur/Tips)

Mammals are warm-blooded animals with body hair and high, internally maintained body temperatures. Females nourish their offspring with milk and, unlike other vertebrates, have three bones in the middle ear – the malleus, the incus and the stapes. Apart from these mammalian basics they are a diverse animal group that includes aquatic, terrestrial and aerial species and many that move between these elements. Some are herbivores, some carnivores and others omnivores. Some are highly social creatures, living in close family groups; others solitary, only meeting to breed. Many mammals have learned to be wary of humankind and are difficult to observe; others are small or nocturnal by habit and so always hard to see. On the other hand some can be quite confiding and, once found, can be watched and photographed with ease.

A wide range of wild mammals is found in central and eastern Europe, representing eight orders. They are the insectivores (Insectivora), which include shrews and moles; the bats (Chiroptera); the land carnivores (Carnivora); the seals (Pinnipedia); the dolphins and whales (Cetacea); the ungulates or hoofed mammals (Artiodactyla); the rodents (Rodentia); and the rabbits and hares (Lagomorpha). The largest land species is the European bison (bulls can weigh over 800kg), and the smallest is the pygmy white-toothed shrew (a whopping 2.5g when wet).

CARNIVORES

There are just 23 species of native carnivore (order Carnivora) in Europe. Seventeen of these occur in central and eastern Europe, compared with just eight in the British Isles. Indeed, the further east one travels across the continent the more meat-eaters are likely to be encountered. From the Baltic States in the north to the Balkans in the south there are not only more species present than in western Europe but they are also usually more numerous. They range in size from the tiny weasel (females often weigh under 40g) to the imposing brown bear (mature males weighing 350kg or more). Some, like the wolf, are highly sociable; others, such as the lynx, lead largely solitary lives.

Wolf cubs (Arco Images/Tips)

Wolf (Gianpaolo Dosio/Tips)

Carnivores possess sharp carnassial teeth, which are ideal for tearing flesh, yet many are omnivorous and overtly opportunistic. For much of the year brown bears are herbivores, eating large quantities of berries, tubers, roots, mushrooms and, of course, honey. Many carnivores are more than willing to feed on carrion, dig for earthworms or steal from smaller predators. In some areas jackals, foxes, martens, badgers and even brown bears roam each night into urban settlements and scavenge for scraps. Carnivores may have evolved for the kill but they are not always up for it.

LARGE CARNIVORES

There are three so-called large carnivores in Europe: namely the wolf, brown bear and lynx. As has happened with other carnivores on the planet, the reputation of these magnificent animals as killers of livestock and game has meant that humankind has persecuted them for as long as anyone can remember. The brown bear and lynx vanished from the UK around 500AD, wolves in the 1700s. Needless

Brown bears can stand 2m tall. (Jiří Bohdal/Naturfoto)

to say, their ruthless reputations are largely undeserved. The lynx has often escaped the worst of this persecution, mainly because of its feline elusiveness. The brown bear, too, has often been spared, probably because humans quickly learned that bears will readily fight back, but the wolf has been less fortunate – mercilessly tracked, trapped and killed across Europe and Asia for centuries. Fortunately attitudes have changed – though there is still work to do – and today these superb species are treated with more respect, and valued and protected in most countries.

Brown Bear *Ursus arctos*

The brown bear is a majestic beast, the largest and most powerful predator in continental Europe, which sits at the very top of the food chain. Adult males can grow to well over 2m tall and weigh 350kg or more. Brown bears are not particularly sociable; males only seek out females in spring and summer when it is time to mate, and do not participate in parental care. Mature females usually have a cub or two in tow; twins are not uncommon. Cubs stay with their mothers for up to four years, but often much less than that, before being driven off. The congregations of bears taking salmon from rivers in North America are the exception, not the rule, and only happen when there is an abundance of food. In Romania similar but less picturesque gatherings occur in some urban areas around rubbish dumps and refuse skips.

Brown bears have been persecuted and hunted for generations and this, together with the development of many of the wild regions they require, has caused them to vanish from most of Europe. No-one knows exactly how many brown bears are left on the continent, but it is clear that the majority live in the Carpathian Mountains, particularly in upland forests in Transylvania in Romania. Two or three population estimates are often available for each country, with the highest figures invariably offered by hunting associations and the more conservative estimates made by

Thick fur keeps out the chill.
(Jiří Bohdal/Naturfoto)

conservation organisations. And herein lies a problem: in most countries a percentage of bears can be hunted (for big money) every year and, the larger the population, the higher the hunting quota. Most official population figures, upon which the quotas are based, are derived from those of national hunting bodies, and tend to be overestimates. For example, in Romania, the population of brown bears is estimated at 4,000–5,000 by conservationists but over 6,000 by hunters. Other countries with viable populations include Bulgaria (500–1,000), Croatia (800–1,000), Estonia (500–600), Slovakia (800) and Slovenia (500–700).

Brown bears are competent swimmers and unsubtle but effective fishers. (Jan Sevčík/Naturfoto)

Though they are certainly strong enough to dispatch a large herbivore, such as a deer, with one swipe of a paw, bears spend most of their feeding time scratching around for much smaller prey and also a lot of vegetable matter. Diet varies between regions and seasons: in spring fresh grass, shoots and bulbs are consumed, replaced later in the year by mushrooms and forest fruits. Roots, honey, carrion, earthworms and insects are taken whenever the occasion arises. In autumn brown bears prepare for hibernation by fattening up on acorns, nuts, beechmast, berries and windfall fruits.

In the Carpathians hibernation may last from November through to March but it is not a deep sleep, rather a torpid slumber, which is interrupted when temperatures are mild. Besides foraging for food some brown bears do actually hunt mammals as big as red deer and wild boar, as well as taking a wide range of smaller animals such as voles, mice and marmots, which are dug out of their burrows. In some regions bears will raid domestic stock, though this is not as widespread a habit as is often suggested.

ENCOUNTERING BROWN BEARS

Much has been written and said about what a person should and should not do when meeting a bear face to face. In most cases nothing at all needs to be done as bears usually do their utmost to avoid humans. However, in the event of a physical confrontation humans stand almost no chance at all, as brown bears are incredibly powerful and fearless. Most confrontations between humans and bears involve animals which have been startled when feeding, or defensive mothers who sense that their cubs are at risk.

- Give bears plenty of respect and space.
- Never run from a bear, instead speak and move your arms to indicate you are human.
- Alternatively, back away slowly and carefully.
- If a bear stands up on its hind legs do not panic, it is merely assessing the situation.
- Never walk directly towards a bear.
- Never approach seemingly 'lost' cubs.
- If a bear moves towards you stand your ground and stand as tall as you can.
- Never look an approaching bear directly in the eye.
- If a bear moves to attack hit the ground face-down and put your hands over the back of the neck.
- When on the ground stay still, silent and 'play possum'.
- Do not climb a tree to escape from a bear unless you are sure you can get above 4m high.

Be careful, it's no teddy bear
(Jiří Bohdal/Naturfoto)

Wolves are highly sociable animals with intriguing family relationships. (Arco Images/Tips)

Wolf *Canis lupus*

The wolf is the largest wild canid (member of the dog family) in the world and the second largest predator in continental Europe. Wolves vary greatly in size and weight, depending upon various factors such as latitude and the prey upon which they feed, but, as a rule those in northern Europe are larger than those in the south. Within all populations males are larger than females, weighing up to 80kg whilst females are rarely over 50kg. Most adults are 1–1.5m long from tip of the nose to tip of the tail – the tail accounts for up to a third of the total length. Wolves are mostly greyish in colour, though some may be silver, rufous or even black, so could be confused with a stray or feral Alsatian-sized dog.

Wolves are very social animals, living in packs, which are essentially large families with a strict hierarchy. Sadly, the days of large packs roaming the countryside are long gone: today a pack may consist of just one family of parents and pups and a couple of juveniles. Within a pack only one dominant monogamous pair breeds: the alpha male and alpha female.

HUNTER AND HUNTED

The preferred prey of wolves is medium to large ungulates such as deer, wild boar and, in the north, elk. Yet they are adaptable and opportunistic animals and, when conditions dictate, will eat much smaller prey such as rodents, ground-dwelling birds or insects, as well as robbing smaller predators of their prey and feeding on any carrion they come across. They also eat a fair deal of vegetable matter. In the natural scheme of things wolves perform the important task of controlling ungulate

Howling wolves: once heard, never forgotten. (Acro Images/Tips)

populations with the old, weak and young taken. The pack usually hunts as a team, though individuals will hunt alone. Such lone wolves cannot bring down larger prey so usually concentrate on the smaller stuff. In some regions wolves prey on livestock and they have done this since humans first began to keep sheep and cattle. Though often exaggerated, this habit is the main reason why mankind has persecuted wolves through the ages.

CRYING WOLF

Is there a more misunderstood wild animal in Europe than the wolf? This intelligent and noble creature has been persecuted for as long as anyone can remember yet, at the same time, it is the ancestor of 'man's best friend', the domestic dog. Up to the end of the 18th century wolves were found throughout most of continental Europe but today only

Sharp eyes, nose and teeth (Photononstop/Tips)

occur in the wildest regions, mainly restricted to montane forested areas even though they are actually better suited to open country. Every country included in this book is home to at least a handful of individual wolves, though there are no precise population figures. Official figures vary greatly and are usually overestimates based on those of hunting associations. A few hundred wolves hang on in Croatia, Estonia, Lithuania, Poland, Serbia, Slovakia and Slovenia Bulgaria is home to some 1,000–2,000 but the European stronghold is Romania. Officially over 4,000 are said to reside in the country, mainly in the Carpathians, though local conservationists believe there may be fewer than 3,000, a figure which translates as around 40% of the European population outside Russia.

WATCHING WOLVES

Wolves are wide-ranging animals, often moving at night and, from experience, have learned to avoid humans. Romania and Bulgaria probably present the best chance of encountering a wild wolf, but one must first get into the right areas, spend some time there and then bank on a fair degree of luck. An alternative is to join an organised wolf-watching tour. Some conservation organisations operate such holidays as part of their educational and fund-raising activities but even joining such a tour does not guarantee wolf sightings. If you are lucky enough to encounter a wolf there is little to fear as there are very few (if any) confirmed cases of them attacking humans.

Europe's largest cat (Bildagentur/Tips)

Lynx *Lynx lynx*

The lynx exudes a typically feline aloofness with its stern expression and impressive long black-tipped tufted ears, which accentuate its noble profile. An adult is around 1m long from the nose to the tip of the stubby tail and stands 50–75cm at the shoulder. It is long-legged, with broad furry paws that come into their own as snow-shoes in winter. The lynx is the most elusive of Europe's three large carnivores and, even when more common locally than wolf and brown bear, is usually harder to observe.

For most of their lives lynxes are solitary and secretive and, except for chance encounters, their presence is often only betrayed by the tracks and signs they leave – claw marks on trees, droppings, scenting posts and tracks. They are mainly silent except when males yowl to declare their presence to females and rival males – this melancholic call is one of the most eerie sounds to emanate from Europe's forests, particularly when heard on cold and crisp winter days. Though it may spook the faint-hearted, there is nothing to fear, and there are no records of lynx ever attacking humans. Indeed, these wonderful big cats seem to go out of their way to avoid people at all costs.

Lynxes are solitary, except for mothers with young kittens. (Arco Images/Tips)

WHAT'S NEW, PUSSYCAT?

The wild forests of the Romanian Carpathians are a stronghold for Europe's largest cat. An official figure of 2,000–2,200 individuals is estimated here, which amounts to about 40% of the total European population. Now the bad news: in recent years a hunting quota of up to 500 lynx per year has been set in Romania, a whopping 25% of the population, or as much as 33% if the figure of 1,000–1,500 that is suggested by conservationists is accepted.

Around 200 are thought to live in Poland, particularly in the Beskydy Mountains in the southeast, and there has been a successful reintroduction into the Kampinoski National Park just west of Warsaw. Lynxes have also been reintroduced into Sumava in the Czech Republic and 100 are estimated to live in the country as a whole. Elsewhere there are 40–50 in Slovenia, 40–60 in Croatia and 350–400 in Slovakia, though, as in Romania, the latter figures are based upon those of hunters and are probably a little optimistic to say the least. It is not clear how many lynx reside in Bosnia-Herzegovina, Serbia, Montenegro and Bulgaria. Further north 1,000 individuals are thought to reside in Estonia, 300 in Latvia and probably around 50 in Lithuania.

During the day, lynx kittens lie low. (Bildagentur/Tips)

In the Carpathians most inhabit old mixed forests above 1,000m where there are good numbers of red deer, wild boar and grouse. At higher elevations chamois are favoured prey and in lowlands hares, roe deer and rodents are hunted. Lynx are mainly crepuscular predators, active at dawn and from dusk into the night, when their exceptional eyesight and hearing, both vastly superior to that of humans, come into their own. Quarry is stalked and ambushed, medium-sized animals dispatched by a clinical bite to the jugular or spine and larger ones grabbed by the throat and suffocated into submission. Kills are dragged to a secluded spot before being partially eaten and then hidden. It is thought that this habit of burying prey under logs, leaf litter, boulders or snow is due to brown bears and wolves regularly robbing lynx of their food. Though lethal predators with sharp claws and incisors, lynx are no match for brown bears or wolves and never challenge them.

MUSTELIDS (MUSTELIDAE)

This family includes weasels, minks, polecats, martens, badgers and otters, all of which are tough, voracious and pugnacious predators which, if need be, can tackle prey larger than themselves. Some are infamous for their ability to release obnoxious odours and liquids – commonly called musk – when threatened. Though, credit where credit's due, they usually give attackers some warning of the treat in store for them, and a chance to back off, by indulging in tail-waving displays before spraying their foul-smelling deterrent. Wise assailants usually get the message. Several members of the mustelid family are seriously threatened and declining in both range and number, which is all the more alarming as they rank amongst the least studied of Europe's mammals.

Larger mustelids, such as the various polecats, often attain the position of top predators in regions where the likes of wolf and brown bear no longer occur. In the past most of these species were frequently trapped for their fur or shot for being 'vermin'. Today, in most places, these two practices are on the wane, but have been replaced by the menace of road traffic.

European mink *Mustela lutreola*

Once widespread in Europe, the European mink is now a rare and endangered species. This amphibious little carnivore has almost totally vanished from western Europe and is now restricted to a few wetlands in the east of the continent. The reasons for this sad situation are not entirely clear, though the loss of the freshwater riverine habitats which they require, and a general degradation in water quality, are probably significant.

In the past European minks were heavily trapped for their fur, but today a more significant factor which has pushed them to the brink is the presence of a close but less-than-welcome relative. The American mink (*Mustela vison*) is a larger, aggressive species, which has rapidly colonised western Europe and moved eastwards after escaping from fur farms. It occupies the same habitats and eats the same prey as the European mink and, when the two species are in direct competition, the smaller native mink invariably loses out. For example, in Estonia, European minks were once widespread but today their American cousins have more or less conquered all the country's mink habitats.

European mink: note the diagnostic white muzzle. (DP)

A small but crucial population of European minks survives on Hiiumaa Island, and a project has been set up to keep it that way. Latvia and Poland are other countries where the pushy Americans are on the increase, whilst the native Europeans haven't been spotted for years. Wetlands that the American mink has not reached, such as the Danube Delta in Romania, are the last European strongholds, though there are fears that it is only a matter of time before things change for the worse here, too, as European minks seem to be declining and there are rumours of American minks being present.

European minks are 30–40cm long, with a bushy tail that is half that length again. They have a glossy, blackish-brownish fur and a cute characteristic white muzzle, formed by a white chin and lips. Most American minks lack white on the upper lip and, if it can be seen, this is a useful, though not diagnostic identification feature. In a nutshell, mink without white on the upper lip are American. Besides being rare, European minks are also mainly nocturnal, solitary and wary, so any views obtained should be cherished – you may never see one again.

The steppe polecat faces numerous threats to its survival in Europe. (TCo)

Steppe polecat *Mustela eversmanni*

Another threatened mustelid is the steppe polecat. It is essentially an Asian species that reaches the west of its range in central Europe, in parts of Hungary, eastern Slovakia, Poland, Romania and Bulgaria. It is a handsome creature, much paler than the more widespread and well-known western polecat (*Mustela putorius*) with a sandy or yellowish coat, dark legs, tail-tip and underparts, and a white face crossed by a black 'lone-ranger' mask. Steppe polecats live in open country, typically on dry lowland steppes where there are colonies of sousliks, mole-rats and hamsters, though they also prey on smaller rodents, reptiles, amphibians and insects. Besides hunting sousliks, steppe polecats will also usurp their burrows and adapt and enlarge them to suit. No rodent in its right mind argues about the eviction. In the recent past the steppe polecat, like most mustelids, was trapped for its fur. Populations also suffered when the use of pesticides to control its rodent prey became the fashion.

Marbled polecat *Vormela peregusna*

Though the steppe polecat is handsome, its close relative the marbled polecat is arguably even more so. Adults are rich brown on the chest, legs and underparts and mottled with a mosaic of brown, yellow, beige and white on the back and flanks. The tail, which is bushier than that of other polecats, is yellowish and ends in a chocolate tip. They have a panda-like face, dominated by a striking broad white band, which crosses the forehead from cheek to cheek, and prominent white-tipped ears. Mature

The striking marbled polecat (EE)

males are particularly good-looking beasts with bright yellow or orange marbling on their backs.

The European range of marbled polecat is the most restricted of the family. Once upon a time they were found in the Carpathian Basin, but today are mainly confined to lowlands in the eastern Balkans. Naturally they are formidable predators and, like steppe polecats, also often live alongside colonies of burrow-dwelling rodents. Anyone lucky enough to corner a marbled polecat may be treated to an impressive warning and defensive display – the tail is splayed out and arched over the body, the head thrown backwards, body hair raised, sharp teeth bared and, if all else fails, a squirt or two of musk is ejected, skunk-style, at the assailant.

Beech martens live happily in both rural and urban areas. (AA)

Beech marten *Martes foina*

The beech marten (also known as stone marten) is widespread across central and eastern Europe, living mostly in low-lying broadleaved woodlands. Though nocturnal, beech martens are often the most easily encountered mustelid as they are also found in settlements, including even busy city centres, where they sleep in buildings. In some local languages they are known as 'house marten' (not to be confused with 'house martin', a familiar bird in the swallow family) and are regarded as pests. They can be noisy, scurrying about and screaming in the attic, and will raid dustbins and burst rubbish bags in the yard. They will even sleep under the bonnets of parked cars – especially in cold winters when the warmth from an engine can be a life-saver – leaving behind bits of food, gnawed bones and droppings and toothmarks on electrical cables and insulation.

The beech marten has a rich brown coat, a long bushy tail and a distinctive white bib, which is indented by a dark stripe from the chest. Its close relative, the pine marten (*M. martes*), is also fairly common but is more of an upland species, inhabiting mature mixed forests. Rarely seen in urban areas, it has a sharper snout, longer and larger ears, longer legs and a fuller yellow bib. Both martens are more arboreal than their polecat cousins, climbing trees with ease and preying on squirrels, dormice and birds, particularly woodpecker nestlings. A quick poke at beech marten droppings will reveal fruit stones and undigested household scraps. Interestingly a close sniff of the droppings of both martens reveals them to be sweeter-smelling than those of other mustelids.

The golden jackal is a versatile predator, equally proficient at hunting and scavenging. (Jan Sevčík/Naturfoto)

OTHER SMALL CARNIVORES

The familiar red fox (*Vulpes vulpes*) is widespread in this region, but there are also less well-known species – the golden jackal and the wildcat. As with the mustelids, these animals can be difficult to observe, often being solitary, nocturnal and always wary of humans.

Golden jackal *Canis aureus*

Of the four species of wild dog (Canidae) found in Europe, the golden jackal has the most easterly distribution. It is actually very widespread, common in the Middle East, Asia and north Africa, and increasing in number and range in southeast Europe. It is quite common in Bulgaria and Romania in dry lowlands and for some years has been quietly heading northwards into central Europe, with recent sightings in the Czech Republic. The golden jackal is a typical dog; it has non-retractile claws, lithe limbs, a long muzzle and sharp teeth, all evolutionary adaptations for hunting and harassing prey in open country. Somewhere along the line however, scavenging for food became an equally important occupation.

Golden jackals are like small, slender wolves, but have shorter legs and more prominent ears. Most adults are about 1m long from nose to tail-tip, with golden or light brown fur. Care should be taken not to mistake a feral dog for a jackal – there are plenty of stray dogs of all shapes and sizes wandering around the Balkans. Golden jackals are mainly active at night but can be spotted by day. Single animals are usually seen, though sometimes a pair of adults or a small pack hunt and scavenge together. Such packs are composed of a dominant pair, a few of their young and one or two non-breeding adult helpers. Everything and anything is seemingly eaten, including titbits from village rubbish dumps.

Wildcat *Felis silvestris*

What is the difference between a cat that has gone 'wild' and a truly 'wild' cat? This question needs to be asked because today truly wild wildcats are few and far between. Persistent persecution by gamekeepers and hunters, who have always seen wildcats as competitors and pests that take game birds, has reduced their numbers in many countries, but an arguably more serious threat to the survival of this woodland-dwelling feline lies much closer to home.

No petting! Wildcats lack the sweet disposition of their domestic cousins. (DT)

The wildcat is the ancestor of the domestic cat. To be precise the first house-cats were individuals of the north African and Middle Eastern race *Felis silvestris lybica*, which was tamed by the ancient Egyptians over 5,000 years ago. To this day the wildcat and its domestic descendants are so closely related that when they meet they mate and together produce fertile offspring. Such hybrids have no trouble successfully breeding with other hybrids, real wildcats or lost pussycats to produce more hybrids. In the end this all means that genetically pure wildcats are endangered.

So when can you be sure you've seen a wildcat and not a fat domestic tabby out for a woodland walk? Or, indeed, a hybrid of the two? Wildcats most resemble grey-and-black tabby cats but are stockier, with a thick bushy tail, which has four or five bold black rings and a thick black tip. Domestics and hybrids have thinner tails, which can be marked with a variety of patterns. True wildcats also lack blotches, spots and mottling, being marked solely with simple dark stripes. Wildcats in the Balkan peninsula are regarded as the most genetically pure in Europe.

HOOFED HERBIVORES

Hoofed mammals are called ungulates. They are divided into two main orders based on the number of toes on each foot: one-toed and three-toed are 'odd-toed' (Perrisodactyla) and two-toed and four-toed are 'even-toed' (Artiodactyla). Europe was once home to two species of wild horses, the continent's only representatives of the order Perrisodactyla. Sadly the European wild ass became extinct in the 1400s and the tarpan followed in its footsteps in the early 1900s. Most of the world's wild ungulates, and all of Europe's, are even-toed and include deer, goats, sheep, bison and pigs. Most of the Artiodactyla are herbivores though the wild boar, Europe's only wild pig, is omnivorous.

WILD BOAR *Sus scrofa*

There are so many gruesome tales about this wild pig that it is a miracle anyone ever dares go out into the woods anymore. Wild boars are indeed big, powerfully built beasts – and males have those famous tusks – but the truth is, the average boar heads off in the opposite direction as soon as it sniffs a human. The main exception to this is a sow with piglets, who will become aggressive if she believes her offspring are in danger.

Wild boar are fairly common in the region's forests. (AA)

The wild boar is Europe's sole representative of the pig and peccary family (Suidae). It is widespread throughout central and eastern Europe, inhabiting broadleaved forests, floodplain woods, reedbeds and even farmland, but can be elusive and difficult to observe. This is partly because it forages at dusk and night-time but also because of its desire to avoid people. Wild boars are omnivores, eating everything from acorns, nuts, tubers and crops to small rodents, earthworms, grubs and carrion. Their rooting and grubbing up of the soil when feeding is beneficial for woodland biodiversity. They have highly tuned senses of smell, hearing and touch (their snout is a superbly sensitive organ) but rather poor eyesight.

Europe's only wild pig (AA)

Females roam in matriarchal bands with juveniles and piglets, which for the first few months have humbug stripes and are as cute as pigs can get. Adult males are bigger than females – standing up to 1m at the shoulder – and are usually solitary, though some form bachelor bands. Mature boars are not particularly sociable, only seeking out sows in autumn and winter when it is time to mate. One of the male's persuasive ploys is to rest his snout on a female's rump and breathe sexually enticing pheromones in her direction.

DEER (CERVIDAE)

There are around ten kinds of deer galloping around Europe today but only three are truly wild and indigenous species: the red deer, the roe deer and the elk. All three occur in central and eastern Europe. For most of the year male deer are instantly recognisable because of their antlers. In some areas artificially high numbers of deer – and wild boar – are maintained and managed by hunting clubs and associations. Hay and other fodder is supplied to ensure a healthy stock of 'trophies' for wealthy clients. This is not always good for the habitat or other wildlife, and predators like wolves and lynxes may not be tolerated as hunting is 'big business' throughout the region.

Red deer *Cervus elaphus*

In central and eastern Europe the red deer is a woodland animal. It is found in mixed forests with glades and clearings where it browses shoots and shrubs and strips many kinds of tree bark – it is particularly fond of spruce. It will also visit fields to graze at dusk and during the night. These forest deer are bigger and heavier than red deer that live on moorland – in Scotland, for example – and stags have more impressive antlers, because a woodland diet is more nutritious. They are fairly common in Poland, the Czech Republic, Slovakia and Hungary, less so in the Baltic States and rather localised in the Balkan countries.

Red deer live in matriarchal herds of related females, immatures and calves. Stags stay aloof and alone for most of the year and take no part in the upbringing or protection of the young. Most hinds give birth to one calf per year, which at first is left alone in thick cover, and only visited when it is time to suckle. Unlike their parents, which have plain, reddish coats, calves are spotted for the first few months of their lives and this basic camouflage is essential.

STUCK IN A RUT

The rutting season begins in September and may last into November. Each dominant stag assembles a harem and fights to defend it from rivals. Besides bodily strength and antler size, the intensity of each stag's bellowing is also an indication of dominance. There is much wallowing in mudbaths, stamping, snorting and flashing of pale rump patches but, if all this fails, stags clash and lock antlers. The aim is not to impale a rival but to push and shove to show who is the strongest.

This red deer hind, suckling its calf, forms part of the stag's harem, which may number up to 20 females. (Jiří Bohdal/Naturfoto)

ANTLERS

Antlers are grown, used and discarded every year, and increase in size and number of points each time. What begins as a pair of prongs in a yearling can end six or seven years later as a fine pair of branched antlers with ten points or more, and measure 80–90cm overall, though the antlers of the oldest stags begin to wane in magnificence. The better the habitat and the nutrition, the bigger a stag's antlers will grow. Antlers start to grow in spring and are covered in a furry skin – known as velvet – which protects and nourishes the bone. By the end of summer the antlers are fully grown and the velvet begins to peel off. Stags speed up this process by rubbing their antlers against trees in preparation for the rut. In spring the antlers snap off at the base but sometimes, when they do not shear simultaneously, stags with one antler can be seen running around like unicorns for a day or two.

Roe deer *Capreolus capreolus*

Roe deer are far more widespread and easier to observe than red deer. From the Baltic to the Balkans the herds of deer sitting right out in the middle of large crop fields by the motorway are invariably roe deer. Such herds are usually composed of does, juveniles, fawns and the odd buck, and may number 100 animals. Smaller groups of bachelors and young females are also formed. The roe deer is small – the largest stand 60cm or so at the shoulder – with an unspotted reddish-brown coat in summer that darkens in winter. It has an attractive face with a black nose, a flashy white backside and a tiny tail. For much of the year bucks – and sometimes does – have small antlers with two or three prongs which grow through the winter, lose their velvet in spring and are shed in the late autumn after the rut. The fawns, usually twins, are darker than adults and spotted and striped white. Fawns are easy prey for predators but their tactic of lying low and keeping still probably means that far more die under the weight of farm machinery.

BARKING MAD

That sudden, loud, bark in the forest is, more often than not, a roe deer rather than a dog. Both bucks and does bark and the noise always seems to sound sharper and louder on crisp winter days. When bucks rub their heads in bushes and on trees they are not scraping off itchy parasites but smearing scent, leaving messages for others, invitations to does and challenges to other bucks. Like all deer they have excellent senses of smell and hearing but their eyesight seems a little suspect. Roe deer quickly spot movement but often stand and stare at stationary objects. It is always wise to keep still and silent when watching wildlife, but especially so with roe deer which can be approached closely if the wind is blowing the right way.

The roe deer family album (from top to bottom): adult female (doe); fawn; adult male (buck) (top & centre FB, bottom DT)

Elk *Alces alces*

Though the elk is the largest deer in Europe it probably cannot be regarded as one of the most handsome. It has a long face, large hairy nose, a drooping upper lip and legs that seem way too long and thin for its body. The long legs have evolved to enable elks to wade with ease through bogs and pools; they end in very large, flat hooves which enable bog-hopping in summer and act as snow-shoes in winter. Elks inhabit wet forests, tree-dotted marshes and floodplains, where they feed on aquatic plants, saplings, tree bark and other vegetation.

A young bull elk with velvet-covered antlers (JP)

Fully grown bull elk sport impressive palmated antlers. (Sunset/Tips)

Adult bulls may stand over 2m at the shoulder and have large, usually palmated antlers. A new set is grown each year in time for the autumn rutting season, then dropped in winter. Each new set of antlers is bigger than the last. Elk are not particularly gregarious: bulls are solitary, whilst females stay in the company of their last calf until shortly before the next one is due, though in winter they form herds led by an old female. Elks are fairly common in the Baltic states and as far south as Poland. A few occasionally turn up in the Czech Republic and these wandering individuals may be instinctively following ancient migration routes that are now largely obstructed by roads, railway lines and other barriers.

Female elk are called cows. (AA)

EUROPEAN BISON *Bison bonasus*

The sad story of this forest-dwelling ungulate (also called the wisent) has a happy ending. Long ago herds numbering thousands thundered across the continent on their migrations to and from seasonal feeding grounds, but gradually the felling of Europe's forests, the race to industrialise and a severe dose of over-hunting all proved too much. By the early 20th century this boreal giant was extinct in the wild. Then, in the 1950s, small numbers were reintroduced from captivity into the old boggy forests at Bialowieza in eastern Poland, where they eventually re-established themselves. Today there are over 3,000 in the wild, mainly in Poland, and as a safeguard, herds have also been placed in other countries and a stock kept in zoos.

There is no mistaking Europe's heaviest land mammal. It is a bulky cow-like animal with heavy, humped shoulders, a rich dark brown coat and two horns, which curve inwards on bulls and are straight on cows. Bulls have a thick woolly mane, can stand almost 2m at the shoulder and weigh up to 900kg. Cows are two-thirds the size of bulls but nevertheless should not be messed with as they are caring mothers and will charge at anything that threatens their calf – calves stay with their mothers for around three years.

Bison are social animals that live in herds of up to 30, usually cows and calves led by an old bull, as well as bachelor bull herds. In late August and September the rutting season begins and bulls bellow, rut up the earth, push and shove and clash horns when defending the cow they have their eye on. Once a bull has mated he wanders off to find another receptive cow. If an old bull is usurped at this time, he usually retires to a solitary life in the forest. Few forest sounds are as melancholic as the deep bellowing of one of these lonely old bulls.

European bison are animals of deep forest (Jiří Bohdal/Naturfoto)

A chamois poses nonchalantly on a near-vertical cliff-side. (Alfred Steiner/Tips)

CHAMOIS *Rupicapra rupicapra*

This agile little mountain goat – the source of 'shammy' leather – spends most of its life above the treeline in Europe's highest mountain ranges, only descending lower in winter when it will also enter forests. Judging by some of the poses chamois adopt as they perch on the very tips of precipitous crags and outcrops, they obviously do not suffer from vertigo. They are seemingly unaware of the laws of gravity, too, as whole families often nimbly hop down and across steep rocky slopes finding steps and footholds where other animals find none. They can jump gaps of 6m, very useful when trying to escape wolves and lynxes – their natural predators.

In summer chamois are light brown with a chocolate stripe down the back but in autumn they shed this coat and become all dark. They have an attractive facial pattern with a dark stripe from the nose across the face and across the eye. Both sexes have long thin horns that curve backwards, ending in a hook at the tip. Males are larger than females, standing up to 80cm at the shoulder. When rutting mature males are very aggressive to younger males, raising the hairs on the stripe on their back and battling with their short hooked horns for the right to mate with females.

There are several places to look for chamois in central and eastern Europe. In Slovenia it is fairly easy to locate them in the Julian Alps; in Poland and Slovakia, in the Tatras, a local race *tatrica* occurs (and graces the emblem of the High Tatras National Park); in Croatia there are herds in the Velebit Mountains; in Romania in the Retezat, Rodna, Apuseni and other ranges; and in Bulgaria in the Rila, Pirin and Stara Planina mountains – the small *balcanica* race is under threat here due to herds living in isolated pockets.

ALPINE IBEX *Capra ibex*

The Alpine ibex was almost lost forever. These magnificent mountain goats have two enemies, avalanches and man and, perhaps predictably, it was man that hunted them to the verge of extinction until, in the 19th century, just one herd of fewer than 40 animals survived in northern Italy. At the 11th hour, a breeding and reintroduction project was launched and subsequently ibex were relocated to zoos and other mountain ranges including the Julian Alps in Slovenia. Today there are thousands of Alpine ibex in the wild, all descended from that one last herd, residing at the highest elevations (over 2,000m) and only occasionally descending below the treeline in spring to graze on fresh shoots. In some areas they are considered to be so numerous that they have been once again placed on the list of game species.

Full-grown males stand almost 1m at the shoulder and are everything a mountain goat should be: hardy, sure-footed with a small 'goatee' beard and magnificent robust horns which are marked with ridges and sweep back over the head. Females have horns too, which – though smaller and less impressive – are used to good effect against anyone or anything that dares threaten their kids. Males only associate with females during the mating season, which begins with a spectacular rutting session in December and January. This involves a 'king of the castle' fight where the largest males leap at one another, clash heads and use their horns to butt each other senseless. Each male jockeys for position, trying to get above its rival to maximise the force of its downwards leaping butts.

Male Alpine ibex have magnificent backswept horns. (MR)

Bechstein's bat is medium-sized, with a stupendous pair of ears. (CF)

BATS

Throughout European history bats have been feared, labelled demonic and even said to be vampires. Yet this negative image is not global; for example, in the Far East bats have always been associated with good luck and prosperity. In modern Europe some of the more irrational ideas about bats have now waned but the advance of civilisation has not seen their lot improve. Climate change, pollution and many of the threats that affect other wildlife have impacted on bats. On a local scale the trend towards illuminating buildings at night, such as historical sites and churches, often disrupts roosting colonies.

Around 45 species of bats (Chiroptera) are found in Europe and over half of these occur in the east of the continent. Several species have the bulk of their population in central and eastern Europe and some only occur here. Blasius' horseshoe bat (*Rhinolophus blasii*) is a little-known species found mainly along the Adriatic and Black sea coastlines, particularly around limestone caves in Slovenia, Croatia, Bosnia-Herzegovina and Montenegro. The long-fingered bat (*Myotis capaccinii*) is also fond of limestone caves but is more widespread, especially in the Balkans. Alcanthoe's bat (*M. alcathoe*) was only discovered in 2001; the core of its range is in the Balkans though it has been found as far north as the Czech Republic and Slovakia. In stark contrast to this tiny species – wingspan just 2cm – is the greater noctule (*Nyctalus lasiopterus*), Europe's largest bat whose open wings span some 46cm. A woodland bat, it roosts in tree cavities and is found from Hungary southwards into the Balkans.

Daubenton's bat hunts over water. (CF)

European free-tailed bat (RV/Bat Conservation International)

The highly mobile and migratory parti-coloured bat (*Vespertilio murinus*) is found from the Baltic States to the Balkans in wooded regions with cliffs. It has adapted to the modern age by sometimes roosting in buildings, even in high-rise apartment blocks in busy cities. Nathusius' pipistrelle (*Pipistrellus nathusii*) is very rare in western Europe but widespread in the east. Another woodland bat, it readily takes to bat-boxes. Savi's pipistrelle (*P. savii*) is found along the Adriatic coast and its hinterland and southern Bulgaria. Schreiber's bat (*Miniopterus schreibersii*) is a cave-roosting bat that has declined severely in the west of Europe; its stronghold is now probably in the Balkans.

FINDING BATS

As a rule there are more bats in the warmer south, but wherever they occur the best time to look and listen for bats is at dusk or during the night. A bat-detector will be needed and wetlands, where flying insects are abundant, are often more productive than dry areas. Cave-riddled regions are often good places to look as many species roost, raise their young and hibernate in caves. Other species are best sought in settlements, where they roost in churches, whilst some are woodland dwellers that roost in tree-holes.

In southeast Bulgaria the rugged Eastern Rhodopes are home to over 20 species, including the European free-tailed bat (*Tadarida teniotis*), a large species with a protruding tail and straight flight which make it one of the easier bats to identify in flight. In Croatia the Paklenica and Krka national parks are perfect locations for bats and bat-lovers. There are 25 species in the Czech Republic and the Palava Hills in South Moravia hosts an impressive 22 of them. The karst landscapes at Aggtelek in Hungary and Slovensky kras in Slovakia together form one cross-border bat paradise – 26 species have been recorded. There are at least 28 species in Serbia and many excellent places to look for them, including two karst regions – around Bor in the east and Valjevo in the west. The gorges along the River Gradac in western Serbia and the River Lazareva in the east are also good sites and very scenic. The Skocjan Caves Regional Park in Slovenia is another superb destination.

Greater noctules are not as ferocious as this picture suggests. (CF)

BATS AND WOODPECKERS

Many woodland bats have evolved to use tree cavities as roosting and nursery sites, but in modern times woodlands often lack the old trees that typically have cavities. This is mainly due to commercial forestry practices such as harvesting trees before they reach maturity. In some places this lack of holes has been addressed by the

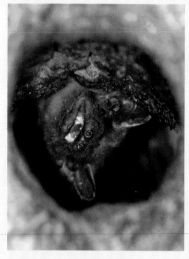

provision of bat-boxes but there is another source of cavities – woodpecker holes. In some areas, such as managed forests where bat-boxes have not been placed, bats may depend upon woodpecker holes for roosting sites. Daubenton's bat (*Myotis daubentoni*), Brandt's bat (*M. brandti*), Natterer's bat (*M. nattereri*), Bechstein's bat (*M. bechsteinii*), common noctule (*Nyctalus noctula*), Leisler's bat (*N. leisleri*), greater noctule (*N. lasiopterus*), common pipistrelle (*Pipistrellus pipistrellus*), Nathusius' pipistrelle (*P. nathusii*), common long-eared bat (*Plecotus auritus*) and barbastelle (*Barbastella barbastellus*) are all known to roost in woodpecker holes and it may well be the case that the distribution of such woodland bats is influenced by the actions of woodpeckers.

Bat using a woodpecker cavity (CF)

INSECTIVORES

The insectivore order (Insectivora) embraces the shrew (Soricidae), mole (Talpidae) and hedgehog (Erinaceidae) families and includes some of the world's smallest mammals. They are ferocious predators, shrews in particular being famous for their voracious appetite for earthworms, slugs, snails, spiders and beetles. Shrews sometimes even tackle and devour other small mammals. The pygmy white-toothed shrew (*Suncus etruscus*) which lives in southern Europe, including Slovenia, Croatia and Montenegro, is one of the world's smallest terrestrial mammals, with a body length of just 35–50mm and a tail of up to 30mm.

Lesser white-toothed shrew (FB)

The eastern hedgehog (*Erinaceus concolor*) is common and widespread east of the Alps and, curiously, the westernmost limit of its range often more or less follows that of the former 'Iron Curtain' where it overlaps in range with the western hedgehog (*Erinaceus europaeus*) – the species found in the British Isles. The two species are very similar in appearance and behaviour and the best way to separate them in the field is to note the eastern hedgehog's pale throat and chest, which contrast with its dark belly. You may see a hedgehog in the very south of the region in winter as they do not hibernate here. Despite their prickly armour of spines, they are preyed upon by martens, badgers and eagle owls, and of course rolling up into a spiny ball is no defence against road traffic.

The eastern hedgehog, like its western counterpart, is a ball of spines. (TT)

RODENTS

The order Rodentia includes mammals as large as beavers and as small as mice. In between there are squirrels, hamsters, voles, rats and dormice, and together these rodents constitute almost 40% of all mammals. The one thing that all rodents have in common is that they gnaw. Whether it's a beaver with a tree or a squirrel with a nut, nothing gnaws quite like a rodent. They have evolved teeth and jaws that have taken this feeding method to another level. There are all kinds of curious species scattered throughout the region, some abundant, others rare, while a few are endemic. Many require a concerted effort and a fair degree of knowledge to find and identify. Specialities include the Balkan snow vole (*Dinaromys bogdanovi*), which as its vernacular name suggests is endemic to the Balkans; the rock mouse (*Apodemus mystacinus*) found along the eastern Adriatic coast and on some Croatian islands; and the pygmy field mouse (*A. microps*), a tiny creature with a body less than 2cm long that inhabits grassy places in the Carpathian Basin and the central Balkans.

Red squirrels occupy all kinds of wooded habitat in central and eastern Europe. (Jan Sevčík/Naturfoto)

above left It looks greyish, but check the ears: red squirrels are quite variable. (FB)
above right The flying membrane is visible on the flank of this flying squirrel. (KW)

SQUIRRELS

There are two basic kinds of squirrel (Sciuridae): those that climb trees and those that don't. The most widespread arboreal species is the red squirrel (*Sciurus vulgaris*), which is fairly common in central and eastern Europe. Despite its name, this species is not always red: many are brown or black. The grey squirrel (*S. carolinensis*), which was introduced into the British Isles from North America and is an alien pest, is absent from central and eastern Europe.

The wonderful little flying squirrel (*Pteromys volans*) is most definitely a native species, one which hangs on in small numbers in some mature, undisturbed spruce and aspen forests in Estonia. It does not really fly but rather glides between trees using baggy membranes of skin between its flanks and legs as 'wings'. When landing it employs these same 'wings' and its long bushy tail as brakes. Flying squirrels are nocturnal, rare and endangered, having suffered badly at the hands of modern forestry methods. Some luck will be needed to see one.

Sousliks are most definitely terrestrial and behave as ground squirrels are supposed to: scurrying about, stuffing their cheeks with food, standing upright, scanning around and diving down their burrows at the slightest sign of danger. There are two species in Europe, both with easterly distributions. The European souslik (*Citellus citellus*) lives in colonies on dry lowland grasslands in the Carpathian Basin, especially the Hungarian Great Plain, and the Black Sea coast. It is a small, slim, sand-coloured squirrel with tiny ears and a short bushy tail. Adults are less than 30cm from nose to tail.

When danger threatens a colony, the sousliks make single, shrill whistles to warn each other. Burrow entrances on flat ground often plunge vertically down and may seem too narrow for their owners to enter, which of course is not the case as they disappear down them at high speed when predators approach. And sousliks must be something of a delicacy as a wide range of predators seek them out: falcons and eagles from the air and storks, cats, dogs and polecats on foot. The spotted souslik (*C. suslicus*) is an even more easterly species that scurries as far west as southeast Poland and eastern Romania. It is

The spotted souslik (*above*, R&MK) has a more easterly distribution than the European souslik (*top*, CF), and can be distinguished by its shorter tail and creamy white spots on the back.

similar to the European souslik, but has a shorter tail and white-cream spots on its back. Both species hibernate during the winter, usually from November to March, though this varies and depends upon local temperatures.

Thick fur and a stocky build help Alpine marmots keep warm in their mountain habitat. (Jiří Bohdal/Naturfoto)

Alpine marmot *Marmota marmota*

This stocky ground squirrel can grow to 70cm in length, which makes it one of the giants of the family. Alpine marmots live on grazed meadows, rocky slopes and boulder-strewn plateaux in high mountains, and are often heard before they are seen as they make sharp whistles to warn their kin when a predator, or hiker, passes by. Good areas include Triglav in Slovenia, the Rodna and Retezat mountains in Romania and the High Tatras in Poland and Slovakia.

Marmots are highly social and live in family groups of up to 20 headed by a dominant pair of adults. Two- and three-year-olds help bring up their younger siblings. Family life centres around a large burrow that is dug into a hillside, often a south-facing slope, and members like to groom each other and rub noses as a greeting. They are diurnal and when above ground at least one individual acts as a sentry, standing upright and scanning for danger.

Young marmots are very playful and will enter the territories of neighbouring families to mix with other young. Adults rarely cross such boundaries as they are territorial and aggressively guard their patch; head females are particularly feisty and will readily fight intruders. Adults mark territories by rubbing their faces against boulders and trees, an action which releases scent from cheek glands. In winter Alpine marmots barricade their burrows with stony debris, earth and grass, and hibernate as a family.

HAMSTERS

Hamsters (Cricetinae) are not the most sociable of rodents. Unlike marmots and sousliks they do not live in colonies, males and females preferring to stick to their own personal burrow. They are assertive little beasts, quick to fight any intruder, using their sharp teeth. Males cross into female territories when it is time to mate, but once finished they are unceremoniously driven off. As anyone who has had a pet hamster will know, these rodents are mostly active at night, though they will come out to feed at dusk. Wild hamsters live in lowlands on dry grassy and stony steppes and fields, feeding on seeds, roots, tubers and insects, which are quickly dispatched and nibbled into oblivion. Food is stored in underground caches and carried there in expandable cheek-pouches.

Alpine marmots love company. (Jiří Bohdal/Naturfoto)

Common hamster
(Miloš Anděra/Naturfoto)

There are three species of hamster in Europe and all are found in the east. The common hamster (*Cricetus cricetus*) is a large heavy hamster, more the size of a guinea-pig than a pet golden hamster. It has an attractive pied coat – sandy or brownish with white and black below – and a short tail. This species is the most widespread hamster and was common across lowland Europe before modern farming forced it from many countries. Today its strongholds are in the Carpathian Basin and Dobrudja. Common hamsters hibernate but wake up to feed from their food caches from time to time. The Romanian hamster (*Mesocricetus newtoni*) has a much more restricted global range, being largely confined to Dobrudja along the Black Sea coast. It looks very much like a pet golden hamster and behaves in a similar fashion, snoozing for most of the day in its burrow and feeding and stuffing its cheeks with seeds at night. The grey hamster (*Cricetus migratorius*) is another eastern species that can be found in the north of the same region. It is more likely to be confused with a vole than another hamster as it is small (half the size of a pet golden) and greyish in colour. Unlike other hamsters it also inhabits wooded steppes and is the only species likely to be seen in mild winters as it does not always hibernate.

Earth-moving equipment: a lesser mole-rat literally chews its way through the soil. (EE)

MOLE-RATS

Mole-rats (Spalacidae) are mysterious mammals. They are totally blind and lead solitary, subterranean lives, constructing a maze of burrows, food stores and dens below the surface and only searching out each other when it is time to breed. They rarely come above ground and when they do it is usually at night. All in all, there is very little chance of coming across a live mole-rat in the wild, though dispersing young sometimes risk a run across open ground during the day. Mole-rats are not related to moles; they are burrowing rodents, but they do have a velvety pelt like real moles. They are about twice the size of a common mole, are grey or brown, lack a tail and their eyes are sunk beneath the skin and sealed by a membrane. A white streak crosses the cheek from the snout to where the eye should be. Mole-rats also lack the powerful paws and feet that moles use for digging, using instead a pair of formidable protruding lower incisors as spades. Mounds of earth (often twice as big as molehills) running across fields often mean a mole-rat is busy below ground.

There are two species in Europe, both inhabiting dry lowland grasslands and steppes in the southeast. The greater mole-rat (*Spalax microphthalmus*) is the larger of the two at up to 30cm long, and eastern Romania is the only place in Europe where there is a chance of encountering it. The lesser mole-rat (*Nanospalax leucodon*) has a slightly wider distribution which includes Romanian and Bulgarian Dobrudja, the Carpathian Basin, especially eastern Hungary, and lowlands in the Balkans.

DORMICE

Lewis Carroll got it right: the one thing all dormice (Gliridae) have in common is their love of sleeping. It has been estimated that some will spend over half their lives snoozing, especially in winter when they hibernate, but also all day long in spring and summer. On the other hand, whoever gave them their English name got it wrong, because dormice are not mice. Another thing all dormice have in common is their reluctance to tread on *terra firma*; many probably never do so during their lives but move around by leaping from tree to tree and using hedgerows as corridors. The common dormouse (*Muscardinus avellanarius*), the smallest species in Europe, looks like a rufous mouse with a furry tail, and is fairly common in central and eastern Europe. The edible dormouse (*Glis glis*) is also widespread and often comes into settlements to hibernate in buildings (as long as they are accessible by trees). It is the largest species and with its long bushy tail might be mistaken for a small grey squirrel.

The furry tail of the common dormouse helps distinguish it from true mice. (CF)

The garden dormouse (*Eliomys quercinus*) is smaller and more rufous in colour, has a black mask around its eyes and below its large ears and a slim tail that ends in a fluffy tuft. The forest dormouse (*Dryomys nitedula*) is much more of an eastern species. It inhabits woodlands from Latvia southwards to the Balkans and as far west as the Czech Republic. It most resembles the garden dormouse though it has smaller ears, a smaller face mask and a longer, bushier tail that lacks the tuft at the tip. Like other dormice it hibernates for months on end: from October to April in the north, for a shorter period in warmer, more southerly countries.

BEAVERS

The European beaver (*Castor fiber*) is the continent's largest rodent. It is a stocky, robust creature with short legs, webbed hind feet, a round head, long yellow teeth and, of course, that famous flat tail. The tail is used as a horizontal rudder and would be unmistakable except that it is often actually hard to see as these aquatic rodents swim very low in the water, with the tail often submerged.

A glimpse of head or tail is often all you will see of a European beaver. (AA)

BUSY AS A BEAVER

European beavers build lodges and dams, but these are rarely as large or obvious as those made by their North American relative the Canadian beaver. Some families prefer to make burrows in banks rather than build lodges and smaller dams are often nothing more than just blocked streams or channels which can be overlooked as they resemble piles of washed-up debris. Felled trees and gnawed stumps and sticks on adjacent banks are, however, a giveaway. Dams and lodges are made from mud, vegetation, branches and the odd larger felled tree trunk, and when they set their minds to it beavers work remarkably quickly and efficiently to finish a job. It is not unusual for dams destroyed by water-workers or anglers to be rebuilt in one night and back in place as good as new the next day.

Dam it all: beaver industry (Jiří Bohdal/Naturfoto)

Beavers live in families of up to six individuals led by a pair of adults. Territories may be linear, along a stretch of river or channel, or based around a pond or lake. Beavers had disappeared from the UK by 1500 but after a history of persecution, hunting and trapping on the continent they have made something of a comeback. There have been re-introductions in several countries as well as natural re-colonisations. In some areas they have even colonised wetlands in urban areas. European beavers are now fairly common in the Baltic States and Poland in wooded lake districts and wide river floodplains lined with softwood trees, such as birch, willow and poplar. Further south they are not as widespread, inhabiting quieter rivers such as tributaries of the Danube in the Czech Republic, Hungary and Croatia.

HARES AND RABBITS

Hares and rabbits are not large rodents, as sometimes presumed, they are members of a quite different order, Lagomorpha. There are over 50 species globally, three of which (in the family Leporidae) occur in central and eastern Europe. The brown hare (*Lepus europaeus*) is the most common and widespread species, and is the famed

Madness? Brown hares frolicking (AA)

'Mad March' hare. Contrary to popular belief the hares doing the best boxing are not rival bucks fighting for dominance but unwilling does fending off over-amorous suitors. These tiffs can happen all year round, not just in March, and are an impressive spectacle.

The mountain hare (*L. timidus*) is also known as the 'blue hare', as a blue tinge from its underfur sometimes shows through its outer coat. It is mainly a northern species, being rare south of the Baltic States. Few European mammals are as well known as the rabbit (*Oryctolagus cuniculus*) but it is not as widespread in central and eastern Europe as in the west, and is absent from the Baltic States and the Balkans.

SEALS

Seals (Pinnipedia) are amphibious mammals, being able to live both on land and in the sea, but they are clearly much more at home in water than on *terra firma*. Evolutionary adaptations such as flippers and thick blubber facilitate a largely aquatic lifestyle and if it wasn't for the fact that female seals have to haul themselves onto the land to give birth they probably wouldn't bother to land at all. Once out of water seals are rather clumsy, vulnerable creatures, so when danger threatens on land they invariably head for the sea, where they are more confident. When breeding it is also very much a case of getting it all over as quickly as possible before going back into the water. Seal milk is very rich and nutritious, allowing pups to grow rapidly and spend a minimum amount of time on land before taking to the sea.

Three species of seal inhabit the Baltic Sea and, weather permitting, can sometimes be seen from aboard the many scheduled ferries that ply the Baltic States and to and from Scandinavia. The common seal (*Phoca vitulina*) is more likely off Poland, often seen lounging around on sand banks in groups of several hundred. When in the water, the common seal's small puppy-like face, with long white whiskers and big kind eyes, is often all that can be seen. The grey seal (*Halichoerus grypus*) is generally found further east off the coastlines of the Baltic States. It is the largest of the

The Mediterranean monk seal is one of Europe's most threatened mammals. (IFAW)

59

three, with adults growing 2–3m long. With its rather flat head, small eyes and a large 'Roman nose' it is, arguably, less attractive than the common seal. The ringed seal (*Phoca hispida*) is the smallest and rarest of the three species and is essentially an Arctic animal, though some reside in the Baltic. It only breeds on ice and can occasionally be seen around Kihnu Island off Estonia. It gets its English name from the many white and grey squiggles and rings that mark its body.

In stark contrast to the three pinnipeds found in the Baltic, the Mediterranean monk seal is a distinctly southern European species. It is also seriously endangered with fewer than 500 thought to survive in the wild, making it one of the world's rarest mammals. It has vanished from most of the northern Mediterranean, with just a few possibly remaining in the most remote areas of the Croatian archipelago. These days sightings along the Black Sea coasts of Romania and Bulgaria, where monk seals used to breed, are few and far between. When visiting these areas it is well worth keeping this rare marine mammal in mind and reporting any observations after making detailed notes. Adults are over 2m in length and dark brown all over except for a white patch on the lower belly, but identification is not a problem as it is the only seal that occurs in these seas. Breeding takes place in undisturbed coves and marine caves. Such places are often popular with divers, boaters and fishermen, causing obvious confrontations and dangers. Pollution, particularly the discharge of untreated sewage into the sea, has added to the seal's plight. Historically monk seals were hunted for their fur or due to perceived competition with local fisheries, though today they are protected in most countries and an international conservation and rescue plan is under way.

CETACEANS

Whales, dolphins and porpoises, order Cetacea, have been hunted throughout the ages. Today they are protected by law in most countries, though pollution of their marine habitats, over-fishing by man, the use of long-line nets and the increase in maritime traffic all continue to threaten many species. Some endemic races, particularly in the Black Sea, are in danger of extinction. The Adriatic coastline of

When it's time to rest, grey seals haul out on beaches and offshore rocks and sandbars. (AA)

Croatia and the seas between its many islands offer the best chance to observe dolphins in the region covered by this book, but it has been observed that dolphins change their behaviour and move to less frequented areas of the Adriatic in the summer boating season. Any cetacean sightings should be reported to the Blue World Dolphin Research Centre on the island of Veli Losinj, quoting date and location (*www.blue-world.org*).

DOLPHINS AND PORPOISES

The common dolphin (*Delphinus delphis*) was the most widespread cetacean in the region, but has declined in number. Groups used to follow boats and ferries in the Baltic, Adriatic and Black seas, though this spectacle (so-called 'bow-riding') is becoming more infrequent. Most adults are around 2m in length, mostly black with pale underparts and conspicuous yellow flanks. The striped dolphin (*Stenella coeruleoalba*) can sometimes be seen in the Adriatic Sea. It is most similar to the common dolphin, but lacks yellow on its sides, being striped grey, black and white instead. The most likely species in Croatian waters is the bottle-nosed dolphin (*Tursiops truncatus*), the familiar dolphin that performs in dolphinariums. It is a social and highly intelligent creature and is widespread, reaching into the Adriatic and Black seas, but not into the Baltic. Those in the Black Sea are an endemic subspecies, *ponticus*, once common but now rare. Historically, large numbers were caught by the various fleets that 'fished' the Black Sea and though this has now largely ceased, the factors which have impacted negatively on all marine life have also affected bottle-noses.

The white-beaked dolphin (*Lagenorhynchus albirostris*) is a northern species that occurs in the Baltic. It is a stocky, rather blunt-nosed dolphin with, as its vernacular names suggests, a white beak. The closely related Atlantic white-sided dolphin (*L. acutus*) is also sometimes spotted in the Baltic, though it is far from common there. Risso's dolphin (*Grampus griseus*) is a large species (adults grow over 3m long) with a heavy build and a blunt, beakless profile. It is mostly grey with darker flippers, flukes and dorsal fin. Adults often appear to have been in cat-fights as they are invariably covered in scratch marks. It is thought that these marks are made by the suckers of squids that did not fancy being eaten and decided to make a deep-sea fight of it. Some Risso's live in the Adriatic and Baltic but are hard to see, as they tend not to follow boats and, when they do, never leap out of the water like other dolphins.

The harbour porpoise (*Phocoena phocoena*) is a member of the Phocoenidae family. It is rather nondescript, being mostly plain greyish with a small triangular dorsal fin and rather small flippers (dolphins have sharp, curved dorsal fins and long flippers). Harbour porpoises used to be common in the Baltic but have recently become rather scarce. Those in the Black Sea are isolated from other populations and belong to an endemic subspecies *relicta* which is in danger of reaching unsustainably low numbers. Unlike most other cetaceans harbour porpoises often come close to shore, even swimming into bays, channels and estuaries and, along with bottle-nosed dolphins, can be spotted from land, particularly from headlands along the Black Sea.

WHALES

The unmistakable killer whale (*Orcinus orca*) is probably the most well-known cetacean of all, the stuff of myths, legends, memorable television documentaries and the star turn in many a marine-wildlife park. Yet the killer whales (aka orca) is not a true whale at all but rather the largest of the dolphins. Adult males can weigh over 5 tonnes and reach over 9m in length; females are smaller at around 6m and newborn young are usually at least 2m long. Small family pods are sometimes sighted in the Baltic, are very rare in the Adriatic and do not enter the Black Sea.

Three species of true whale are occasionally sighted in the Baltic: the northern bottle-nosed whale (*Hyperoodon ampullatus*), minke whale (*Balaenoptera acutorostrata*) and sei whale (*B. borealis*). None is numerous and there are certainly better places in the world to go whale-watching. Cuvier's beaked whale (*Ziphius cavirostris*) occurs in the Adriatic, but is rarely seen alive; most specimens have been found washed up onshore. It is a deep-sea feeder that can dive to almost 2km and remain submerged for over an hour. The fin whale (*Balaenoptera physalus*) is very occasionally sighted in the Croatian Adriatic.

Bottle-nosed dolphins are often seen in the Adriatic and Black seas. (LS)

BIRDS

European bee-eater (DP)

Central and eastern Europe is quite simply superb for birds and for birdwatchers. There are plenty of 'eastern' specialities that rarely, if ever, venture into the west of the continent and some superb spectacles: thousands of red-breasted geese in winter, waves of white storks moving down the Via Pontica in September, hordes of common cranes in Hungary in October and noisy colonies of red-footed falcons, to name just a few. Besides these 'sexy' species, there are also many other birds that, though they do occur in the west, are far more abundant and easier to find in the east. Species like black stork, little crake, white-backed woodpecker, river warbler, red-breasted flycatcher and lesser grey shrike come to mind.

WETLAND BIRDS

The region is absolutely flooded with aquatic habitats. Lakes, bogs, marshes, rivers and manmade reservoirs and fishponds support a vast array of birds.

FISH-CATCHING SWIMMERS

Two species of diver (Gaviidae), also known as loons, are commonly found on passage and in winter. Both the black-throated diver (*Gavia arctica*) and red-throated diver (*G. stellata*) head south via rivers like the Danube, hopping from landlocked wetland to wetland, before spending their winters on the Black and Adriatic seas. A few black-throated divers also breed in the very north of the region in Estonia. Grebes (Podicipedidae) tend to inhabit shallower and more vegetated wetlands than divers. In spring all five European species indulge in elaborate courtship displays with plenty of splashing and shaking of heads. The Slavonian grebe (*Podiceps auritus*) breeds only in the very north (despite its name it does not breed in Slavonia), and the red-necked grebe (*P. grisegena*) has the most eastern distribution of the family.

Europe's two pelican species (Pelecanidae) are very much eastern birds. The bulk of the continent's white pelicans (*Pelecanus onocrotalus*), some 3,500 pairs, breed in Romania's Danube Delta. The rarer Dalmatian pelican (*P. crispus*) is seldom seen in Dalmatia (though a few reside on Lake Skadar in Montenegro) preferring wetlands along the Black Sea coast. White pelicans usually fish in flocks, working together to herd and scoop up shoals, whilst Dalmatians tend to fish alone.

Dalmatian pelicans may gather on shallow inland lakes but, unlike white pelicans, tend to fish alone. (JP)

Cormorants (Phalacrocoracidae) have a bit of an image problem: even keen birdwatchers often ignore them and anglers positively hate them. The exception is possibly the pygmy cormorant (*Phalacrocorax pygmeus*) which is abundant in the Danube Delta.

LONG-LEGGED WADING BIRDS

Most herons and egrets (Ardeidae) are lanky wading birds that will stand in water and 'freeze' for what seems an age before suddenly stabbing with their long dagger-like bills into a passing fish or frog. The squacco heron (*Ardeola ralloides*), purple heron (*Ardea purpurea*) and great egret (*Egretta alba*) often nest in noisy, mixed colonies in the south of the region.

Though close relatives, the white stork (*Ciconia ciconia*) and black stork (*C. nigra*) could not behave more differently when it comes to nesting. White storks place their bulky nests on telephone poles and rooftops, whilst black storks seek out secluded woodland spots and build their nests against the trunks of large trees. Approach an occupied white stork nest and the birds will pose for photographs; walk towards a black stork nest and the sitter will slip silently away. Quite how one stork became so tolerant of humankind, while the other became so shy and suspicious, is something of a mystery.

Occasionally, ornithologists get it right and give a bird a name that fits. A good example is the spoonbill (*Platalea leucorodia*), a bird that actually has a spoon-shaped bill, which it uses to sift and spoon up molluscs and crustaceans from soupy waters. There are large reedbed colonies of spoonbills in Hungary and around the Balkans.

SKULKERS

Rails and crakes (Rallidae) are often overlooked. The little crake (*Porzana parva*) is fairly common on wetlands with thick reed and rush beds. At around 18cm long, it is often hard to spot as it creeps around the edges of reedbeds. Baillon's crake (*Porzana pusilla*) is often even harder to find as it is even smaller, mostly nocturnal and prefers wetlands where there are billions of mosquitoes.

A wealth of wetland birdlife (*from top*): a pygmy cormorant drying its wings (MV); a squacco heron in flight (JP); white storks guarding their rooftop nest (KP); the shy black stork (JP); a spoonbill showing off its most famous feature (KP).

The corncrake (*Crex crex*) is a rail that avoids overly wet habitats, preferring instead to go about its business in damp hayfields, pastures and iris beds. In spring its rasping, buzzing 'song' can be heard from the Baltic to the Balkans.

TERNS

The black tern (*Chlidonias niger*), white-winged tern (*C. leucopterus*) and whiskered tern (*C. hybridus*) are known as marsh terns. All three are small, dainty birds that hawk over freshwater for flying and swimming insects. Marsh terns breed in colonies, building their flimsy nests on floating vegetation. In breeding plumage the white-winged tern is a very attractive 'pied' tern, which is fussy about which marshes it nests upon. In some years large numbers breed in Poland, in others in eastern Hungary, but everything depends upon spring water levels.

SMALLER WETLAND BIRDS

Many passerines use wetlands, including some striking and endearing species. There are two distinct races of bluethroat (*Luscinia svecica*): the red-spotted *svecica* and the white spotted *cyanecula*. In each case the spot is placed at the centre of a brilliant blue bib. Interestingly, the two races live in very different wetland habitats: white-spotteds nest in reedy lowland wetlands, while red-spotteds inhabit wooded upland bogs.

The penduline tit (*Remiz pendulinus*) is a petite bird that weaves a sock-shaped nest from rush and willow seed-heads. This delicate enclosed construction hangs (hence the *pendulinus*) at the end of a thin twig, usually over water in a willow or birch tree, and has a spout-shaped entrance, which is thought to deter snakes and other predators.

In recent years the citrine wagtail (*Motacilla citreola*) has started to establish itself as a regular breeding bird on wet meadows and sewage farms in Poland and the Baltic States. Hold your breath and take in its bright lemon plumage.

More wetland birds (*from top*): corncrake in full voice; a dapper white-winged black tern; bluethroat collecting food for its chicks; a dazzling male citrine wagtail (all MV)

66

WILDFOWL

The wetlands of the region host huge numbers of swans, geese and ducks (Anatidae) on both spring and autumn migration. In April, Matsalu Bay in Estonia attracts around 350,000 wildfowl, including whooper swans (*Cygnus cygnus*), Bewick's swans (*C. columbianus*), barnacle geese (*Branta leucopsis*), white-fronted geese (*Anser albifrons*), bean geese (*A. fabalis*) and masses of diving, dabbling and sea ducks. From November to March almost all of the world's red-breasted geese (*Branta ruficollis*) reside along the Black Sea coast in Romania and Bulgaria, grazing the vast winter wheat fields by day and roosting on lagoons by night.

The European stronghold of the ferruginous duck is in the east. (MV)

At about the same time the shallow sea off the Baltic States sees rafts of Steller's eider (*Polysticta stelleri*), which come down from their Arctic breeding grounds. Some species also breed in the region, most notably the endangered ferruginous duck (*Aythya nyroca*), which has strongholds in Hungary, Croatia and Romania. In breeding plumage drake red-crested pochards (*Netta rufina*) look outrageous with their bouffant orange heads and crimson bills.

Large flocks of red-breasted geese winter along the Black Sea coast. (DT)

The drake Steller's eider is a stunningly attractive sea-duck. (JP)

SEABIRDS

Boat and ferry trips on the three seas that fringe the region are often the best way to get close to seabirds, though seawatching can also be done from headlands in the Baltic States and Bulgaria. Cory's shearwater (*Calonectris diomedea*) and Yelkouan shearwater (*Puffinus yelkouan*) can be seen skimming along in low lines over both the Adriatic and Black seas, sometimes close to shore. Skuas (Stercorariidae) are gull-like predatory birds that have perfected the art of piracy on the high seas. They are particularly adept at harassing terns and auks, forcing them to drop or disgorge fish. A wide range of gulls (Laridae) can be seen all year round. The rarest, and one of the most attractive, is Audouin's gull (*Larus audouinii*) which in recent years has started to nest on rocky islets off the Croatian islands of Lastovo and Mljet.

Audouin's gulls (AJ)

GRASSLAND BIRDS

Weighing up to 25kg, adult male great bustards (*Otis tarda*) are among the world's heaviest flying birds. They are not the tallest, nor do they have the widest wingspans, but they are bulky and need several running steps before they can launch themselves into the air. Great bustards have declined almost everywhere, including central and eastern Europe, where they have been unable to cope with modern farming methods. The exception is Hungary, where a core population is protected. In spring males gather in leks, puffing out their chests, turning their tails inside out, and generally strutting their stuff to impress watching females.

Common cranes (*Grus grus*) are tall, elegant birds that breed in the wooded bogs and wetlands of the north. They are long-distance migrants, heading south every autumn to winter in Africa. Up to 100,000 congregate on the grasslands and croplands of eastern Hungary each October, where they refuel, leaving only when the first winter frosts arrive. Both adults are devoted parents and escort their young (one or two chicks is the norm) on this long journey, making bugling calls whilst the young reply with high-pitched whistles.

Stony hillsides are the home of the chukar (*Alectoris chukar*) and rock partridge (*A. graeca*), two closely related birds that are best separated by range of occurrence. The former is found in the south and east of the Balkans, whilst the latter is common in Croatia and as far north as the Alps. Where they overlap in range, identification is something of a problem! The stone curlew (*Burhinus oedicnemus*) is not a true curlew at all but Europe's only thick-knee (Burhinidae), a family of big-headed, large-eyed birds that creep around arid grasslands in the Balkans and as far north as Hungary.

The great bustard is one of the world's heaviest flying birds and a striking sight on the Hungarian *puszta*. (DT)

Red-backed shrike (JP)

Some perching birds (passerines) have taken up a more terrestrial lifestyle, often preferring to feed and nest in grassy places. These include shrikes (Laniidae), various larks (Alaudidae), pipits and wagtails (Motacillidae), buntings (Emberizidae) and wheatears (genus *Oenanthe*). Steppes and grasslands in eastern Bulgaria and Romania are home to two rare species of wheatears: Isabelline wheatears (*Oenanthe isabellina*) use souslik burrows as nest sites, whilst pied wheatears (*O. pleschanka*) inhabit slightly lusher areas, sometimes at the edge of settlements.

Pied wheatear (JP)

With their hooked bills, shrikes are, in effect, mini raptors. They are the infamous 'butcher birds' that impale prey on thorns. The lesser grey shrike (*Lanius minor*) is often conspicuous as it sits on roadside wires adjacent to grasslands, waiting for insects and small mammals to move on the ground below. Arguably the most striking of the family is the masked shrike (*L. nubicus*), which haunts more cultivated areas in the southeast Balkans. The red-backed shrike (*L. collaris*) is another handsome species.

The common crane is a stirring sight, whether migrating overhead (*main picture* JP), dancing on the ice (*inset left* MV) or facing down a fox (*inset right* MV).

A wallcreeper is the ultimate prize for mountain-climbing birdwatchers. (DT)

MONTANE BIRDS

The high peaks, moors and forests of the Tatras, Carpathians and other ranges are home to a fascinating mixture of birds. Alpine swifts (*Apus melba*) breed in colonies on rock faces and in gorges in the southern Carpathians. Europe's largest swift, with a 50cm wingspan, Alpine swifts are often seen zooming by in aerial formation while making twittering and screaming calls. The crag martin (*Ptyonoprogne rupestris*) establishes its colonies in gorges, caves and sometimes in road tunnels and on hotel walls. The Alpine accentor (*Prunella collaris*) is an often unobtrusive passerine that breeds at the highest elevations, on screes and boulder-dotted plateaux in Slovakia, Slovenia and the Balkans. Isolated populations of shore larks (*Eremophila alpestris*) breed on barren ground above the treeline in the Balkans. This bird gets its English name from its habit of visiting coasts in winter, and is also known as 'horned lark' due to two black feathers that protrude from the head of breeding males.

The nutcracker (*Nucifraga caryocatactes*) is an arboreal crow, found in mountains were there are stands of conifer laden with seed-filled cones. It is often easy to see in autumn, particularly in ski resorts, when birds fly to and fro hoarding pine cones and hazelnuts for the winter.

ON THE ROCKS

Many alpine birds have adapted to finding a living on sheer rock faces. The rock thrush (*Monticola saxatilis*) and blue rock thrush (*M. solitarius*) are two close relatives found in rocky places in the south of the region. The former is migratory and breeds as far north as Hungary, the latter is resident and confined to the southern Balkans. The rock nuthatch (*Sitta neumayer*) hops and flits around limestone walls in the Balkans. It nests in wall crevices, reducing the size of the entrance to suit by plastering it up with mud.

Alpine choughs (*Pyrrhocorax graculus*) are also often confiding and sometimes willing to join in the *après-ski*. They inhabit rugged uplands as far north as the Alps, swirling above cliffs and through gorges in flocks.

The crimson-winged and enigmatic wallcreeper (*Tichodroma muraria*), the sole member of the Tichodromadidae family, is a cliff-dwelling species that birdwatchers drool over. It breeds in high, rocky regions in the Balkans and Slovakia, but it is not always necessary to hike up and through tough terrain to see one, as they drop down to lower elevations in winter, residing in quarries and even on the walls of castles and cathedrals.

top Nutcracker (MV)
above Rock thrush (MV)

The delicate camouflage of a hazel grouse makes it extremely hard to spot. (MV)

FOREST GROUSE

Though actually fairly common in mature mixed forests in the Baltic states, Poland, Slovakia and the Balkans, the hazel grouse (*Bonasa bonasia*) can be a very hard bird to see. It is quick to flush, either running into dense cover or flying up into the canopy when stumbled upon. Often, just a whirring of wings is heard and nothing seen, though in spring cocks will hop onto rocks or logs and raise their crown feathers in display whilst making high-pitched whistles. When lekking, black grouse (*Tetrao tetrix*) and capercaillie (*T. urogallus*) are also impressive birds, but sadly not as common as they once were. Their strongholds remain in the old boreal forests, though isolated populations hang on in undisturbed pockets in the Carpathians.

BIRDS OF PREY

There are around 33 regular species of diurnal raptors (birds of prey that fly by day) in the region. Most are highly efficient predators with sharp talons and beaks, a few are solely scavengers, and some are expert at both methods of getting a meal.

SCAVENGERS

The griffon vulture (*Gyps fulvus*) breeds in scattered cliff colonies in the Balkans. It is a huge bird, with a 2.5m wingspan, that soars effortlessly over arid, open country. The black vulture (*Aegypius monachus*) is even larger (wingspan up to 2.85m), but today is very rare, only occasionally patrolling the skies over the Eastern Rhodopes in Bulgaria. The Egyptian vulture (*Neophron percnopterus*) is much smaller, with a wingspan of up to 1.7m, but more widespread than its larger relatives. The practice

The magnificent and powerful white-tailed eagle (MV)

of lacing bait-carrion with poison, in an attempt to 'control wolves and other vermin', almost wiped out vultures in the Balkans. Thankfully this misguided behaviour is now outlawed and has largely ceased.

The white-tailed eagle (*Haliaeetus albicilla*) is often referred to as 'sea eagle', but this is misleading as the species lives quite happily on many landlocked, freshwater wetlands. Despite its massive beak and formidable talons, this eagle is essentially a scavenger, feeding on dead fish and just about anything else that has passed away or is on the verge of it. Some live prey is caught, with pond terrapins being a favourite.

HAWKS, BUZZARDS AND HARRIERS

Hawks (accipiters) are woodland birds which employ a rather different hunting technique from harriers. Rather than patiently patrolling the ground for prey, hawks use speed and power to ambush or chase down other birds in flight. The secretive Levant sparrowhawk (*Accipiter brevipes*) nests in broadleaved woodlands in the Balkans and migrates southwards in autumn to the Bosphorus. Levants are more likely to prey on ground-dwelling animals, such as lizards and insects, than other hawks, but otherwise surprisingly little is known about their ecology.

There are three species of true buzzard (genus *Buteo*) in Europe. The common buzzard (*Buteo buteo*) is indeed common, the larger rough-legged buzzard (*B. lagopus*) is essentially a boreal species which winters in the south and the long-legged buzzard (*B. rufinus*) is mainly confined to the Balkans. Though their breeding ranges do not overlap, with careful timing, and a little luck, all three buzzards can be seen on the same day, for example in autumn in eastern Hungary or Romania.

Harriers are slender, graceful raptors, typically seen gliding low over open country.

top Griffon vultures nest in busy colonies on craggy cliffs. (AA)
above Juvenile eastern imperial eagle (MV)

The hen harrier (*Circus cyaneus*) is badly named as it mostly hunts small mammals. This bird is a short-distance migrant, breeding on moors and bogs in the north of the region and wintering in the south. Not quite as common, Montagu's harrier (*C. pygargus*) is a summer visitor that hunts over grasslands and farmland where there is plenty of small prey to pounce upon. The marsh harrier (*C. aeruginosus*) is common and widespread and more attached to wetlands than its close relatives.

EAGLES

For many people eagles are the epitome of power and prestige and this has sometimes commanded them respect when other raptors have been persecuted. Despite having hooked bills and sharp talons, eagles sometimes seem to be rather over-equipped for the hunting job, as they often feed on small prey such as hamsters, voles, lizards and insects and never turn their beaks up at carrion. Nine species from five genera breed in the region. Two species, the eastern imperial eagle (*Aquila heliaca*) and greater spotted eagle (*A. pomarina*), are very much eastern birds, the kind that birdwatchers will travel long distances to see. The eastern imperial eagle breeds in low numbers in the Balkans, eastern Slovakia, the Czech Republic, Serbia and Hungary, its European stronghold. The greater spotted eagle is even rarer, nesting in forested wetlands in the Baltic States and eastern Poland. The closely related and very similar lesser spotted eagle (*A. pomarina*) is much more widespread.

top The saker is the largest falcon in the region. (JP)
above Female red-footed falcon (MV)

FALCONS

Falcons (Falconidae) are small to medium-sized raptors with slim bodies and pointed wings. They are swift fliers that mostly tackle prey on the wing. Nine species regularly occur in the region, including some decidedly eastern specialities. Red-footed falcons (*Falco vespertinus*) are gregarious, often hunting in hovering bands for insects and small mammals, and nesting in colonies in open country. They depend largely upon corvids for nests as they (in common with other falcons) do not construct their own. Adult males are stunning, with smoky bluish-grey bodies, silvery flight-feathers, rusty trousers and orange-red feet and bills. Eleonora's falcons (*F. eleonorae*) arrive back from their wintering grounds somewhat later than other migrants and only begin to breed in July, nesting on island sea-cliffs in the Adriatic and raising their young in late summer. At this time passage songbirds that are moving south over the sea provide abundant prey for the agile falcons.

The saker falcon (*F. cherrug*) is a raptor conservation success story. After decades of decline, due to pesticide use, egg collecting and the robbing of chicks for the falconry trade, this powerful falcon has recently made something of a comeback. Pairs are dotted around the southeast of the region with a core population of around 150 pairs in Hungary's lowlands. Sakers are built to take medium-sized birds like doves, pigeons and shorebirds and mammals such as hamsters and sousliks, but they are also not averse to stealing prey from other raptors.

SHOREBIRDS

Shorebirds or waders (Charadriiformes) are terms used to group together a range of birds from several families that feed in, or by, water, usually by wading and probing with their long beaks. Most nest on the ground, though a few nest in trees. A good range of these birds breed, pass through and winter in central and eastern Europe. There are species that will be familiar to birdwatchers from all over Europe, like the avocet (*Recurvirostra avosetta*), lapwing (*Vanellus vanellus*) and curlew (*Numenius arquata*), but also others that rarely head west to the Atlantic coast.

Collared pratincole (MV)

One of the best habitats for migrating shorebirds is the drained fishpond. Every autumn the majority of these innumerable manmade wetlands have their water pumped out when the fish are harvested. The resulting muddy basins are magnets for flocks of stints, sandpipers, godwits, shanks and plovers. Rarer species such as the broad-billed sandpiper (*Limicola falcinellus*) and marsh sandpiper (*Tringa stagnatilis*) often drop into such places. The Terek sandpiper (*Xenus cinereus*) is a curious shorebird that runs with a forward-leaning stance and has a slightly upturned bill. Small numbers turn up on drained ponds through the region and a few sometimes breed at the Nagli fishponds in eastern Latvia, and this is as far west as it gets. The collared pratincole (*Glareola pratincola*) is an elegant flier that looks and behaves more like a tern than a typical shorebird, taking insects on the wing and diving around whilst making harsh, high-pitched calls. They breed in colonies in the south of the region, inland or on the coast, on lakesides, paddyfields, marshes and saltpans.

PUTTING ON A SHOW

Ruffs (*Philomachus pugnax*) breed in bogs and wet grasslands in the Baltic States and pass through the whole region in large flocks in both spring and autumn. This species is unusual in having two different English vernacular names for the sexes: ruff for males, reeve for females. When heading north in spring, males are in their extravagant and variable breeding plumage, complete with the Shakespearean ruff (a generous frill of colourful feathers) around the neck. Keen to breed, they stop off to display to one another at traditional lekking sites, which means lots of posturing and flapping about, as well as the odd bit of pecking and kicking.

above Great snipe (MV)
below Male ruff displaying (DT)

Another lekking species is the sought-after great snipe (*Gallinago media*), a secretive inhabitant of wet meadows and bogs in Poland and the Baltic States. On spring evenings males gather at traditional lekking grounds to display, which involves standing upright, often on tussocks, and making strange bubbling and clicking noises.

OWLS

Owls (Strigiformes) are nocturnal hunters with exceptional vision and fine-tuned hearing. There are ten regular breeding species in the region, all resident except for the migratory scops owl (*Otus scops*) which winters in Africa and the south of the Mediterranean. Scops owls range as far north as Slovakia and the Czech Republic, inhabiting open woodlands, orchards and parks, but they are much more common in the Balkans where the large insects they prey upon are abundant. The 'song' of the scops owl is a repetitive *tuu... tuu... tuu* whistle, which can last all night long and irritate even the most devoted owl lovers.

The eagle owl (*Bubo bubo*) is a formidable predator and, at up to 70cm long, the largest owl in Europe. It preys upon a wide range of birds and mammals, but most specialise in locally abundant small animals such as hedgehogs or rats. Those living by wetlands will take roosting grebes, coots, ducks and gulls. Eagle owls typically nest on cliffs and in stone quarries but in forests, where rocky places are lacking, they will use raptor or black stork nests or even incubate on the ground beside a log or rock.

At the other end of the scale is the pygmy owl (*Glaucidium passerinum*), which despite its size (under 20cm), is a fierce crepuscular hunter, with an angry facial expression to match. Pygmy owls inhabit upland coniferous and mixed forests and are cavity breeders though, unable to excavate their own nest holes, they rely upon woodpeckers for nesting sites. In spring the male's song, made at dawn and dusk, is a piping whistle, not unlike that of the scops owl but higher pitched. In autumn a series of ascending notes, called 'the ladder', is made. These calls are often the first indication that pygmy owls are present.

Pint-sized pugilist: the pygmy owl is a ferocious hunter (JP)

Tengmalm's owl (*Aegolius funereus*) also lives in forests and relies upon woodpeckers for nest sites. Slightly bigger than the pygmy owl, it prefers black woodpecker cavities and will use a favourite hole for many years. Tengmalm's owls are highly nocturnal and hunt for voles, their main prey, by listening for movement. Another much larger forest owl is the Ural owl (*Strix uralensis*). This long-tailed woodland hunter is more diurnal than its relatives and in winter can even be seen in the middle of the day, sitting out in clearings, waiting patiently for potential prey to move. Ural owls, with their small black eyes and relatively unmarked faces, lack the ferocious facial expression typical of most owls, but this is misleading as they will vigorously defend their owlets from any human threat.

The Ural owl's mild expression belies a fearsome nature. (MV)

The white-backed woodpecker is rare and declining. (MV)

WOODPECKERS: THE CARPENTERS

There are ten species of woodpecker (Picidae) in Europe and all occur in the region. Nine are resident and can be seen all year round, whilst the migratory wryneck (*Jynx torquilla*) arrives in early spring and departs for Africa in late summer. This travelling lifestyle is not the only thing that separates the wryneck from its relatives: it perches like a songbird, doesn't drum and is unable to excavate nest holes. Woodpeckers have evolved a range of morphological adaptations that make them the undisputed carpenters of the forest: robust chisel-like bills for hacking into timber, powerful neck muscles, strong stocky legs and claws for gripping vertical surfaces and stiff tail feathers that act as props.

The impressive, crow-sized black woodpecker (*Dryocopus martius*) is Europe's largest woodpecker and is common throughout the region. Black woodpeckers are able to hack out cavities in the sound timber of large living trees; most woodpeckers, including blacks, are rather lazy and choose the soft option of a tree with heart-rot. Many other birds (stock dove, various owls), mammals (pine marten, dormice) and insects (wasps, hornets), which are themselves unable to excavate, rely upon black woodpecker holes for homes. The grey-headed woodpecker (*Picus canus*) is a close relative of the perhaps more familiar green woodpecker (*P. viridis*). Both of these birds like to spend time on the ground, lapping up ants with their long sticky tongues, though the grey-headed is less terrestrial than the green and usually prefers more wooded areas.

The Syrian woodpecker (*Dendrocopos syriacus*) is mainly a bird of secondary

The powerful black woodpecker is an
efficient tree surgeon. (MV)

lowland habitats such as orchards, vineyards, parks and gardens and rarely enters forests proper. Around 100 years ago Syrians hopped into Europe from Turkey and started to expand their range northwards. They are now common in the Balkans and reach as far west as the Czech Republic and as far north as Poland. Always take a good look at any Syrian woodpeckers encountered, as they occasionally interbreed with great spotted woodpeckers (*D. major*), producing hybrid young which show plumage features from both parents.

The middle spotted woodpecker (*D. medius*) is mainly tied to oakwoods. Unlike most woodpeckers it is almost completely monomorphic (both sexes look basically the same). The white-backed woodpecker (*D. leucotos*) is the continent's rarest species and an inhabitant of old-growth forests with plenty of rotting timber. It has disappeared from most of western Europe. The lesser spotted woodpecker (*D. minor*) is another lover of broadleaved woodlands with lots of dead wood. This tiny woodpecker (15cm long) avoids competition with its larger relatives by feeding in the canopy, gleaning insects from the smallest twigs and leaves, where other woodpeckers are unable to tread. The three-toed woodpecker (*Picoides tridactylus*) is mainly found in old forests of spruce, pine and fir. This secretive and often silent woodpecker likes to visit recently burnt forests, where it gorges itself on the beetles that infest the dead trees. As one would expect, three-toed woodpeckers have just three toes on each foot, unlike its relatives which all have four.

The inconspicuous but vocal river warbler (JV)

WARBLERS

The warbler family (Sylviidae) embraces several genera of small, often rather skulking birds, many of them good songsters. These 'LBJs' (little brown jobs) include scrub warblers (*Sylvia*), reed warblers (*Acrocephalus*), warblers with insect-like songs (*Locustella*), tree warblers (*Hippolais*) and leaf warblers (*Phylloscopus*). There are around 30 breeding species in our region, including several eastern specialities. The barred warbler (*Sylvia nisoria*) is common and widespread in dry, scrubby habitats, whilst the orphean warbler (*S. hortensis*) is a more southern species.

The aquatic warbler (*Acrocephalus paludicola*) is an endangered bird with very precise wetland habitat requirements: grazing marshes in Hungary and sedge beds in Poland and the Baltic States. The paddyfield warbler (*A. agricola*) is essentially an Asiatic bird that taunts birdwatchers from reedbeds along the Black Sea coast. The mechanical and monotonous cicada-like buzzing 'song' of the river warbler (*Locustella fluviatilis*) is often the first, and sometimes only, indication of its

above left The barred warbler is big, bold and loud. (MV)
above right The aquatic warbler is one of Europe's rarest birds. (ML)

presence. It is another eastern species, common in swampy, bushy places from the Baltics to Romania. The icterine warbler (*Hippolais icterina*) is the most widespread of the so-called tree warblers, whereas the olivaceous warbler (*H. pallida*) gets no further north than Hungary. The olive-tree warbler (*H. olivetorum*) is a large warbler which hides in oakwoods, orchards and, of course, olive groves, in Dalmatia and the southern Balkans. Much smaller, and found much further north, the greenish warbler (*Phylloscopus trochiloides*) demands sharp eyes, patience and mean identification skills to track down.

The greenish warbler is one of several tiny leaf warblers, best distinguished by song. (MV)

A SPLASH OF COLOUR

Several unrelated birds in the region stand out as being rather colourful, even a tad exotic-looking. They are mostly migratory, embellishing the region in spring and summer, but wintering in warmer climes. The azure, green and orange kingfisher (*Alcedo atthis*) is found wherever there is a combination of clean running water and sandy banks in which to burrow a nest chamber. Unlike in Britain, most central and eastern European kingfishers move southwards in winter when their waterway homes freeze over. The bee-eater (*Merops apiaster*) is many people's favourite (bee-keepers apart), being multi-coloured and superbly acrobatic in flight. When the roller (*Coracias garrulus*) 'rolls' in flight on a summer's day, its turquoise, blue and rufous plumage is a sight to behold. However its call – a harsh, crow-like *rak-ack* – is as ugly as it gets.

top Rose-coloured starling (MV)
centre Bee-eater (MV)
below Black-headed bunting (JV)

A hoopoe contorts itself into the best sunbathing posture. (DT)

Two rollers reveal stunning colours as they get amorous. (MV)

Though male golden orioles (*Oriolus oriolus*) are a stunning combination of bright yellow and black, they have an uncanny knack of blending in with tree foliage. This oriole's liquid, fluty song is one of the sounds of summer. Another bird with striking black and yellow plumage is the black-headed bunting (*Emberiza melanocephala*), a fairly confiding songbird that likes to sit out on wires and other exposed perches in scrubby and bushy country in the Balkans. In most years large flocks of rose-coloured starling (*Sturnus roseus*) invade from Asia. The usual procedure is that they arrive in late May, swirl around the region's lowlands searching for insect prey and, in years of grasshopper and locust abundance, establish noisy breeding colonies in June.

REPTILES

Green lizard (DP)

Herpetologists (people who study reptiles and amphibians) are seldom without something to watch or photograph in central and eastern Europe. The Balkan countries in particular are home to snakes and lizards that do not occur anywhere else in Europe. In reptile hot-spots several similar species of snake and lizard can be found living side by side. They are able to coexist in close proximity because they are utilising the habitat and its resources in subtly different ways. Though there is overlap, the various species are feeding on very particular prey (in terms of size and type) and hunting at different times. Each species is in fact a specialist.

The majority of reptiles are diurnal (active by day) but they are seldom on the go all day long. When looking for reptiles remember that they need heat in order to be active, but at the same time they must avoid over-heating. In summer many reptiles are active in the morning and early evening, but rest during the middle of the day, when temperatures are at a peak. Earlier and later in the year these same species may be most active in the midday hours and less so in the cooler mornings and evenings. In winter, when temperatures are constantly low, most species hibernate. Fortunately these periods of reptile activity often fit in nicely with that of the average travelling reptile watcher.

TORTOISES

Two of the three species of tortoise (Testudinidae) that occur in Europe are found in the region covered by this book. Hermann's tortoise (*Testudo hermanni*) is by far the most widely distributed, occurring in lowlands across the Balkans as far north as Croatia – which is as far north as any wild tortoise gets in Europe. Any tortoises seen in Slovenia are probably descendants of escapes from the commercial trading that used to occur between Yugoslavia and western Europe. The spur-thighed tortoise (*T. graeca*) has a more limited range, living in coastal Romania and Bulgaria and in dry lowlands along the lower Danube. The two species are very similar in appearance but the spur-thighed is larger – the shell length of adult females often reaches 25cm, whilst Hermann's is seldom over 20cm. As its name suggests the former also has

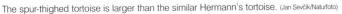

The spur-thighed tortoise is larger than the similar Hermann's tortoise. (Jan Ševčík/Naturfoto)

spurs on the backs of its thighs, which Hermann's lacks. Being slow-moving creatures tortoises are, once found, easy to observe and photograph, though they should never be handled or removed as in some areas they are under pressure from illegal collection for the pet trade.

TERRAPINS

Terrapins (Emydidae) are aquatic reptiles and are rarely seen on land. Any terrapin encountered on *terra firma* – females lay their eggs on land – can easily be distinguished from a tortoise by its flat shell. They are essentially carnivores, preying on insects, amphibians and small fish, whereas tortoises eat vegetation. The most common and widespread species is the European pond terrapin (*Emys orbicularis*), which can be seen basking on logs, rocks and floating vegetation in freshwater lowland wetlands from Latvia southwards to the Balkans. Adults can grow to 30cm (shell length) but most are smaller than this. They are typically blackish in colour, with subtle yellow spots on the head and faint streaks on the shell.

The closely related Balkan terrapin (*Mauremys rivulata*) is confined to the southern Balkans, reaching as far north as southern Bulgaria, Montenegro and Dalmatia. It looks very much like its relative but is paler, lacks spots on the head and has stripes on its neck.

LIZARDS

Sorting out the many lizards (Lacertidae) found in central and eastern Europe can be a challenge. Lizards may allow prolonged observation when basking in the sun, but more often than not they dive for cover when approached and can be very tricky to photograph. It is worth remembering that range of occurrence can be a useful aid when trying to identify one of these 'now-you-see-it, now-you-don't' reptiles. Learning to recognise the common wall lizard (*Podarcis muralis*) can be the basis for identifying others. The Balkan wall lizard (*P. taurica*) is also fairly widespread, being common in Hungary and the southern Balkans. The Italian wall lizard (*P. sicula*) is in coastal Slovenia and Croatia, while the Dalmatian wall lizard (*P. melisellensis*) occurs from Slovenia southwards along the Adriatic coast. However, Erhard's wall lizard (*P. erdhardi*) is uncommon and only likely to be seen in the very south of the region.

top European pond terrapin (PM)
above Dalmatian wall lizard (FB)

The viviparous lizard (*Laceta vivipara*) is a widespread and variable little lizard found over most of Europe and Asia. Females usually give birth to fully formed young (hence the 'viviparous') but in some areas lay eggs like most other lizards. The meadow lizard (*L. praticola*) is another species that in Europe is found only in the Balkans, though it is also rather localised here, living in lightly wooded hill country in Serbia, Romania and Bulgaria.

Three small endemic rock lizards that keener herpetologists will want to get to grips with are Horvath's rock lizard (*L. horvathi*), Mosor rock lizard (*L. mosorensis*) and sharp-snouted rock lizard (*Podarcis oxycephala*). All three will probably require some hill trekking to find as they are upland-dwelling species, though the sharp-snouted is possible at sea level. Horvath's rock lizard is endemic to damp karst uplands in Croatia and Slovenia, Mosor rock lizard lives in wet mountain habitats, often above the treeline, in Dalmatia, Bosnia-Herzegovina and Montenegro, whilst the sharp-snouted rock lizard is more restricted in range, only living in the very south of Croatia, Montenegro and Bosnia-Herzegovina.

The steppe runner (*Eremias arguta*) is an eastern lizard that just creeps (or runs) into the region along Romania's Black Sea coast and dry areas in the Danube Delta. It is a stocky, greyish lizard, flecked with paler marks and stripes. The largest specimens can reach 15cm from the snout to the tip of the tail. As its name suggests it is a speedy lizard that darts for cover when disturbed. The global range of the Dalmatian algyroides (*Algyroides nigropunctatus*) is limited to the Balkan coastline and hinterland of the Adriatic, where it inhabits dry rocky and bushy places. It is a dark brown or rufous, short-bodied but long-tailed lizard – maximum 20cm in length, of which two-thirds is tail – with orangy underparts and flanks. Adult males have a striking turquoise throat. The Balkan green lizard (*Lacerta trilineata*) is a larger version of the more widespread green lizard (*L. viridis*). The former is found from coastal Croatia and Romania southwards, whilst the latter occurs across much of

southern and central Europe. Where they overlap in range, they can be very difficult to separate, though mature male Balkan green lizards have yellowish throats, whilst green males have bluish ones. While much smaller – often half the size of the above two species – male sand lizards (*L. agilis*) are also often green on the flanks and sometimes all across the back.

The sand lizard is a small, attractive and widespread lizard. (FB)

above The Dalmatian algyroides is a fleet-footed Balkan speciality. (LB)
below The Balkan green lizard has an exceptionally long tail. (Luboš Mráz/Naturfoto)

The slow worm is the most widespread 'legless' lizard in the region. (Jiri Bohdal/Naturfoto)

LEGLESS

Two lizards that have no choice but to slide like snakes are the slow worm (*Anguis fragilis*) and European glass lizard (*Ophisaurus apodus*), as these are both legless. Slow worms occur over much of Europe but the glass lizard is only found in the Balkans, mainly in dry coastal regions from Croatia and Romania southwards. Adult glass lizards are unmistakable, unique and impressive creatures that reach 140cm in length (slow worms are rarely more than 50cm). They have a distinct groove running down the side of their body and often show the protruding remnants of hind legs.

SKINKS

There are over 1,000 species of skink (Scincidae) worldwide, but just ten in Europe. The snake-eyed skink (*Ablepharus kitaibelii*) is the only species in this region, found mainly south of central Serbia and southern Romania, with an isolated population in northern Hungary and southern Slovakia. It is a small (maximum 13cm long) ground-dwelling animal fond of warm, dry lowland and hilly areas, often with light woodland cover. Snake-eyed skinks lack eyelids and though they have legs (unlike some other skinks), they often prefer to slither along like a snake.

The snake-eyed skink is serpentine in appearance. (EE)

Kotschy's gecko is not as adept a climber as some of its relatives. (LB)

GECKOS

Geckos (Gekkonidae) are the best climbers in the lizard family. Their toes end in strong claws and some have adhesive pads that enable them to scale even the smoothest of surfaces, even windowpanes. They are often found on buildings where they hunt for insects attracted to lamps. The Moorish gecko (*Tarentola mauritanica*) and Turkish gecko (*Hemidactylus turcicus*) are common around the Adriatic. The creature seen scurrying vertically up the balcony wall or across the ceiling, when you're on holiday, is invariably one of these. Kotschy's gecko (*Cyrtopodion kotschyi*) is mainly found in the southern Balkans and the Bulgarian Black Sea coast, where it lives in rocky terrain on walls, cliffs, ruins and buildings. Though obviously a good climber, the Kotschy's toes lack adhesive pads and this is probably why it does not readily scale the heights achieved by its close relatives.

Moorish gecko: look out for this lizard on your hotel balcony (Bruno Manunza/Tips)

The large whip snake, like all its family, is a slender and agile creature that sometimes climbs into low foliage. (MM)

SNAKES

In many societies snakes provoke fear and loathing and are associated with bad luck or even the devil. This is all rather sad as they are fascinating creatures that are essentially harmless. There are a dozen species of typical snake (Colubridae) in the region. The grass snake (*Natrix natrix*) and smooth snake (*Coronella austriaca*) occur throughout, the former in wetlands, the latter usually in drier habitats. The large woodland-dwelling Aesculapian snake (*Elaphe longissima*) and the water-loving dice snake (*Natrix tessellata*) can be found from the Czech Republic southwards. Most other species – the Montpellier snake (*Malpolon monspessulanus*), Dahl's whip snake (*Coluber najadum*), western whip snake (*C. viridiflavus*), Balkan whip snake (*C. gemonensis*), large whip snake (*C. jugularis*), four-lined snake (*Elaphe quatuorlineata*), leopard snake (*E. situla*) and cat snake (*Telescopus fallax*) – occur in the Balkans.

TWO ODDITIES

The worm snake (*Typhlops vermicularis*) is a curious reptile found in Dalmatia, Bulgaria and Montenegro. If you are lucky enough to come across one, take a good look before it slips away because you will be watching arguably the strangest snake in all of Europe. It hardly looks like a snake at all, resembling a large (30–40cm) shiny brown worm with tiny eyes and a head that is smaller than the tip if its tail.

There are around 80 species of boa (Boidae) in the world but only one, the European sand boa (*Eryx jaculus*), occurs in Europe – in dry sandy, stony, country in Bulgaria and southern Romania. Unlike its tropical relatives – anacondas and pythons – it is small (maximum 80cm long) and harmless. European sand boas are viviparous, that is, they do not lay eggs but give birth to live young.

The four-lined snake can reach nearly 2m in length (PM)

Some of these snakes are common in countries such as Croatia, Montenegro and Bulgaria, but that does not mean they are easily found and observed. The fact that most snakes are inactive for several months of the year when hibernating and then inactive for long periods during the day in summer, when it is too hot, means that they are often elusive.

The nose-horned viper (*above*, Luboš Mráz/Naturfoto) shares the zigzag patterning of the more widespread adder (*below*, R&MK), but can be distinguished by the distinctive horn on its nose.

VIPERS

Vipers (Viperidae) are typically rather stout snakes with blunt heads and snouts and vertical pupils. All three species found in the region use stealth, rather than speed, to hunt small mammals, lizards and insects. The adder (*Vipera berus*) is the only viper over much of Europe, including most of central and eastern Europe. The nose-horned viper (*V. ammodytes*) on the other hand is restricted to the southeast and Balkans. It is the only snake in the region with a horn on the tip of its nose which, together with its triangular head and vertical pupils, creates a somewhat menacing look. Indeed, this snake should not be messed with as its venom – injected through 1cm-long fangs – is highly potent (see below). The meadow viper (*V. ursinii*) seldom strikes or bites and its venom is not as strong as that of the nose-horned. It is the smallest of the three species, adults usually measuring 50cm long, and preys mostly on crickets and grasshoppers, though it will not turn its nose up at small lizards or rodents. Meadow vipers are endangered across their range, today surviving in isolated population pockets in Hungary and the Balkans.

VIPERS AND VENOM

All the vipers found in the region are venomous but they pose little threat to humans, unless provoked. Vipers are generally placid creatures that like to be left alone, though voles and mice may disagree! Most viper bites are not life-threatening to humans (victims of bites from meadow vipers have compared them to a bee-sting) but people react to bites in different ways. In most cases there is a burning sensation, numbness, swelling and localised pain. Sometimes vomiting and diarrhoea occurs and, in extreme cases, shock and death may follow.

- Knowledge and prevention are the keys to avoiding getting bitten.
- Vipers should be respected, observed from a distance and never prodded or picked up.
- When looking for vipers or simply walking in viper country wear long trousers and boots.
- Advise children and ask them to stay on paths.
- Keep dogs on a lead.
- In the event of a person being bitten find a local doctor as soon as possible. In a national park or reserve locate a ranger as they may have experience of viper bites and/or medical training.
- Keep the victim calm.
- Immobilise the area bitten.
- Do not apply a bandage or any pressure to the area bitten.
- Do not offer any medicines or drinks (only water) until professional help is obtained.

AMPHIBIANS

Marsh frog (DP)

Amphibians are excellent indicators of environmental health. Newts, frogs and toads are often the first animals to disappear when there are problems in the local environment. Sadly there are many cases across the globe of once common amphibians declining and even vanishing altogether. Habitat loss, drainage schemes, pesticide and fertilizer use, introduction of alien species and water pollution are just some of the factors which negatively affect amphibians. Yet there are places in central and eastern Europe where these animals are still doing well. One of the best locations to see amphibians is the Danube Delta in Romania where at least 20 species occur.

Many amphibians leave their aquatic breeding homes in the autumn and head for lush woodlands, where they hibernate through the winter under logs and stones, in crevices and in leaf litter. They return in spring when the breeding season beckons.

Unlike true toads, common spadefoots and their relatives have vertical pupils. (DP)

The bright markings of the fire salamander are thought to deter predators. (FB)

SALAMANDERS

Two species of salamander (Salamandridae) occur in the region. The fire salamander (*Salamandra salamandra*) is a striking creature with its rubbery black skin and bright yellow spots and streaks. There can be considerable variation in the pattern and extent of the yellow and some may be marked red or orange. Others are unmarked and there are also regional differences. Just as with zebras and tigers, no two fire salamanders have the same pattern. This bright colour warns potential predators that things might not be as tasty as they seem. If a predator fancies a salamander snack and ignores this visual message the salamander secretes a poisonous fluid from paratoid glands behind its eyes and will even squirt this into the face of the attacker. These glands resemble bulbous eyebrows. Adults can be up to 25cm long from snout to the tip of the tail, though most are smaller. Fire salamanders occur from southern Poland south into the Balkans, in damp upland forests, usually deciduous, and by clean water sources such as streams or ponds, which they need for breeding. They are mainly nocturnal, hiding during the day in leaf litter or under logs or stones. The best time to see them in the daytime is often just after a period of rainfall, when they crawl out and cross otherwise dry surfaces such as roads in search of slugs. Despite their bright patterns they can be remarkably difficult to spot when in leaf litter, but, once found, fire salamanders are usually easy to observe and photograph as they are placid and sluggish.

The Alpine salamander (*S. atra*) is a rare species found in high mountain ranges in central Europe and the Balkans such as the Julian Alps in Slovenia and the Dinaric range in Croatia, Montenegro and Bosnia-Herzegovina. It inhabits damp deciduous and coniferous forests, and also meadows above about 800m. Individuals living at the highest altitudes may spend up to two-thirds of the year in hibernation. Alpine salamanders (up to 15cm long) are smaller than fire salamanders and lack the yellow markings of their relative, being totally black.

Alpine newts live in the Carpathians and Balkan ranges, as well as the Alps. (FB)

NEWTS

Newts (Trituridae) are voracious aquatic predators that grab and devour tadpoles, insects and even adult damselflies that come too close to the water surface. Despite its vernacular name the Alpine newt (*Triturus alpestris*) is not always found at high elevations. In Poland and the Czech Republic, for example, this species occurs at quite low levels. Alpine newts exhibit neoteny (a condition where amphibian larvae do not necessarily metamorphose into adults but continue to grow and are sometimes able to breed and reproduce young). The Italian crested newt (*T. carnifex*) may have an identity crisis, since not only is it found in Italy but also in Slovenia, Croatia, Montenegro and Bosnia-Herzegovina. It is also neotenous and those that do metamorphose into adults breed with other *Triturus* species. The Carpathian newt (*T. montandoni*) is indeed only found in the Carpathian Mountains, though even here it is localised – in Romania in the eastern Carpathians, in Poland and Slovakia in the Tatras and in the Czech Republic in the Beskydy. It is also known as Montandon's newt. The Balkan crested newt (*T. karelinii*) is a large, impressive species (females can be up to 16cm long) found mostly in high mountains in southern Serbia and Bulgaria. By contrast the Danube crested newt (*T. dobrogicus*) is a lowland species and true to its name lives mainly in the Danube Basin.

MINIATURE MERMAID

The olm (*Proteus anguinus*) has been called the 'human-fish' and indeed would not be out of place in an H G Wells novel. This strange and fascinating troglodyte is the only member of the Proteidae found in Europe. It is a salamander that never develops from larval to adult stage but which can breed and produce young – a classic case of neoteny. Olms can grow to a length of 30cm, are usually white or greyish with external pink feathery gills, stunted limbs and tiny eyes that lie under the skin. In caves in Bela Krajina in Slovenia there are black olms, and dark individuals are also found where subterranean waters near the surface. The olm is endemic to karst caves with underground wetlands in the Dinaric Alps in Slovenia, Croatia, Montenegro and Bosnia-Herzegovina. The only place in the world where wild olms can be seen with any certainty is in the Postojna Caves in Slovenia. Here guided tours pass pools, which contain a few of these remarkable amphibians.

The bizarre and mysterious olm (AB)

FROGS AND TOADS

By far the largest amphibian group, frogs and toads are also, in general, the easiest to observe.

TRUE FROGS

The frogs of the family Ranidae (typical frogs) can be conveniently divided into two groups: green-coloured and brown-coloured. The greens are very aquatic, raucous and include the marsh frog (*R. ridibunda*), pool frog (*R. lessonae*) and edible frog (*R. kl. esculenta*). The noisy marsh frog is the largest native frog in Europe – adults regularly attain 16cm. Most are olive or brown with dark spots and blotches on the

Male marsh frog with inflated vocal sacs (FB)

back and flanks. When males are in full 'song' their exposed vocal sacs are grey, and noting this is a good way of separating smaller males from pool frogs, which have white vocal sacs. When a marsh frog chorus of '*brek-brek-brek-kek-kek-kek*' starts up in spring, all other frogs are drowned out. Pool frogs are similar to marsh frogs but smaller, sometimes half the size. They are widespread and common from Estonia to the Danube valley. The edible frog is a hybridogenetic form (the result of inter-breeding between marsh and pool frogs) hence the 'kl' in the scientific name, which means '*klepton*' and indicates a hybrid. Though composed of hybrids, populations of edible frogs are maintained because females mate with male pool or marsh frogs to produce young. Male edible frogs are, as it were, unable to contribute further. Edible frogs are common in wetlands north of the central Balkans, the south of the range coinciding with that of the pool frog. The Albanian pool frog (*R. shqiperica*) is similar to the pool frog and can be seen in coastal Montenegro.

The brown group is composed of the common frog (*Rana temporaria*), moor frog (*R. arvalis*), agile frog (*R. dalmatina*) and Balkan stream frog (*R. graeca*) all of which are more terrestrial and less vocal than the greens. The moor frog is very much a central and eastern European species but does not occur south of northern Croatia and central Romania. Most live in lowland wetlands though relic populations exist in upland pools and bogs. It is a stocky, short-legged frog, which varies in colour from buff to grey to brown. Breeding males may turn bluish for a short period in spring. The agile frog is a woodland dweller found from southern Poland southwards into

Male moor frogs turn blue to impress females. (TT)

True to their name, agile frogs perform long leaps to escape predators. (KP)

the Balkans. It has a distinctive large brown ear patch and a yellow hue on the groin. And it is very agile, using its long slim legs to make long leaps when disturbed. Balkan stream frogs are typically found by running water in uplands in the southern Balkans. They are less elegant than agile frogs, with blunter snouts, an indistinct ear patch and a dark throat.

TREE FROGS

There are four species of tree frog (Hylidae) in Europe and they are the only amphibians on the continent that regularly climb trees and other vegetation.

Common tree frog calling (FB)

The common tree frog (*Hyla arborea*) is the most widespread tree frog, though it has declined in the west and today has its core population in the east, occurring in all the countries included in this book except Estonia. It is a small, cute frog with slim limbs and a smooth, almost rubbery skin. The tips of the toes end in broad, gecko-like sticky pads. Adults reach 5cm in length with females slightly bigger than males. Most are light, bright green, though skin colour can change according to background and temperature and can be olive or brown. On each flank there is a dark stripe that runs from the eye to the hind legs. Males differ from females in having a dark vocal sac on the throat, which is inflated when 'singing'.

Outside the breeding season common tree frogs are not very aquatic and may be seen far from water and often quite far from trees: in fact they avoid thick forests, often living in reedbeds and scrub. They do however need fresh water for breeding – temporary lakes and pools, drainage channels, ditches and even cart-tracks that have filled with water are all used. On summer evenings and, especially, at night, a loud, raucous chorus of *krak, krak, krak* is repeated in bursts by males. For such a small creature the noise is remarkable and many males may gather and compete for hours on end. If you are lucky enough to find a pair copulating you will see that the male grasps the female under her armpits rather than around the loins, the norm for most other frogs.

BOMBINA TOADS

The fire-bellied toad (*Bombina bombina*) is found in lowland wetlands from Latvia in the north to Bulgaria in the south. This is a small, dark toad with reddish blotches and spots on its underparts which serve to warn predators of a toxic secretion that is emitted from the skin. When attacked, fire-bellies may flip onto their backs to reveal these bright markings, but they do not always do this, presumably because they have not read the right herpetological literature! In summer their distinctive calls can be heard during the day, but it is during warm nights that the noise created

above left Like other *Bombina* toads, the fire-bellied toad has a nondescript upperside. (PM)
above right The bright flipside of a yellow-bellied toad (TT)

by multitudes of these creatures in unison is at its most impressive. At close range each toad's gentle piping *poo-poo-poo* can be heard but from a distance, when innumerable males compete, this becomes an incessant humming.

In uplands the fire-bellied is replaced by the yellow-bellied toad (*B. variegata*), a slightly larger and paler animal with yellow to orange belly markings that continue onto the thighs. This species also has a more westerly and southerly distribution, and is rare north of the Tatras. Good areas to search for yellow-bellies are the Carpathians and Balkan ranges, where they reside in pools, slow-moving streams, puddles and water-filled wheel-tracks. Yellow-bellied toads make similar piping noises to their close relatives, though the '*poos*' are more like '*poops*' and the cacophony is arguably more musical.

When conditions are right, yellow-bellied toads may breed three times a year. (TT)

above Although they need water for breeding, at other times green toads can tolerate much drier conditions than most other toad species. (all FB)

TRUE TOADS (BUFONIDAE)

The green toad (*Bufo viridis*) is an endearing little amphibian, which likes to approach streetlamps, enter houses and shower-cubicles in campsites in search of insects attracted to lights. It is absent from most of western Europe but widespread in lowlands in the east. Similar in build to the common toad (*B. bufo*) but smaller (females reach 10cm, female common toads 15cm), they are also more attractive, being marked almost all over with a mazy pattern of greenish blotches. Green toads have a high-pitched trilling 'song' that is more likely to be mistaken for a cricket than another amphibian. The smaller natterjack toad (*B. calamita*) occurs from the Baltic States southwards as far south as the Czech Republic. In can be heard on warm summer nights making its nightjar-like churring in coastal heaths and dunes.

Common spadefoot toad: widespread and feisty (Jan Sevčík/Naturfoto)

SPADEFOOTS

There are three spadefoots (Pelobatidae) in Europe, two of which are eastern species: the common spadefoot (*Pelobates fuscus*) and eastern spadefoot (*P. syriacus*). Both are lowland amphibians, highly nocturnal with large bulbous eyes and usually inactive by day except during the breeding period. Spadefoots have vertical pupils, which immediately separates them from all other frogs and toads in the region. The name refers to the large protruding spur on each hind foot, which is used as a spade for digging burrows. Spadefoots are stocky with short legs and blunt heads, all

Eastern spadefoot toad: confined to the southeast of the region (Miloš Anděra/Naturfoto)

adaptations for excavating. The common spadefoot is the more widespread of the two, being found in lowlands – often in sandy places like dunes, grasslands and crop fields – from Estonia southwards to the northern Balkans. When molested it can be a feisty little beast, puffing itself up, rocking on its hind legs and even leaping with its mouth open at any threat – all bravado as it is harmless. The eastern spadefoot is confined to the very southeast of Europe, in lowland Bulgaria, the south and east of Romania and parts of Serbia.

INVERTEBRATES

A cicada wing (DP)

though often less obvious to our eyes, invertebrates (animals without backbones) are far more diverse and numerous than vertebrates, and are every bit as fascinating. Central and eastern Europe offers a rich hunting ground for anyone interested in insects, arachnids, molluscs and the many other flying, crawling, burrowing and swimming creatures that play such a crucial role in supporting the more glamorous beasts higher up the taxonomic order. Space permits only a general look at the more striking invertebrates of the region, as a taster of the riches awaiting discovery.

BUTTERFLIES

Whether you are a serious lepidopterist (someone who studies butterflies and moths) or one of the growing number of amateur enthusiasts, central and eastern Europe will not disappoint. Across the

The intricately marked map butterfly *Araschnia levana* (FB)

region there are plenty of skippers (Hesperiidae), whites and yellows (Pieridae), coppers, blues and hairstreaks (Lycaenidae), fritillaries and vanessids (Nymphalidae) and browns (Satyridae). Since butterflies love the sun, timing and destination are important. June to August is the best period to observe them on the wing and, as a rule, the number of species increases as one heads south – Estonia has around 111 regular species, Hungary 166 and Croatia 186, while over 200 occur in Bulgaria. (There are only 56 native butterfly species in the British Isles.)

Unmistakable and widespread: the Camberwell beauty *Nymphalis antiopa* (FB)

The eastern festoon is one of the region's most sought-after insect jewels. (EE)

FULL OF EASTERN PROMISE

A real attraction for the listing lepidopterist is the eastern species which do not occur at all in western Europe. The southern swallowtail (*Papilio alexanor*) is a large, beautiful butterfly, which can be seen from late April to July along the Croatian coast. The eastern festoon (*Zerynthia cerisy*) can sometimes be seen as early as March in southern Romania, southeast Serbia and Bulgaria. A somewhat trickier species to find and identify is the Balkan green-veined white (*Artogeia balcana*), a very localised butterfly in the southern Balkans. The eastern greenish black-tip (*Euchloe penia*) is essentially a Middle Eastern species that occurs at the northernmost point of its range in the Pirin Mountains in Bulgaria.

A complex group to separate are the clouded yellows: the moorland clouded yellow (*Colias palaeno*) flies over acidic bogs from the Baltic States as far south as Slovakia; the Danube clouded yellow (*C. myrmidone*) is, true to its name, found in countries through which the Danube flows, as well as in Poland and the Czech Republic; whilst the Balkan clouded yellow (*C. caucasica*) is localised in Bosnia-Herzegovina, Montenegro and Bulgaria. The lesser clouded yellow (*C. chrysotheme*) and eastern pale clouded yellow (*C. erate*) are two Asian species that flutter into Europe in parts of Poland, Hungary, Slovakia, Romania and (the latter) Bulgaria.

The only place in Europe to look for Nogel's hairstreak (*Tomares nogelii*) – one of Europe's least-known butterflies – is the Dobrudja Plain in Romania. The Balkan copper (*Lycaena candens*) is an upland species in Montenegro, Serbia and Bulgaria. Then there are the 'blues': the eastern short-tailed blue (*Everes decoloratus*) is found

Dainty, but eye-catchingly bright, the Balkan copper favours upland meadows. (MM)

in Hungary, Slovenia, Serbia, Romania and Bulgaria; the blue argus (*Ultraaricia anteros*) in mountains in Croatia, Montenegro, Romania and Bulgaria; the anomalous blue (*Agrodiaetus admetus*) is very local in Hungary, Croatia, Bosnia-Herzegovina, Serbia and Bulgaria; and the false eros blue (*Polyommatus eroides*) is in Poland, Slovakia, Serbia and Bulgaria.

Freyer's purple emperor (*Apatura metis*) is an attractive species found in riverine woods along the Danube and its tributaries from southern Hungary to Bulgaria. The Hungarian glider (*Neptis rivularis*) is, inevitably, found in Hungary but also in neighbouring countries. To see the yellow-legged tortoiseshell

The Danube clouded yellow is found along the river that shares its name. (FB)

(*Nymphalis xanthomelas*) in Europe one has to visit Slovakia, southern Poland or Romania, though it is far from common. Another predominantly Asian butterfly is Pallas's fritillary (*Argynnis laodice*), which occurs from Latvia to Romania, but only as far west as Slovakia. The eastern rock grayling (*Hipparchia syriaca*) reaches as far north as Dalmatia. The Bulgarian ringlet (*Erebia orientalis*) is an endemic, found only in Bulgaria's higher mountains, the black ringlet (*E. melas*) is scattered at high elevations in the Balkans, whilst the Dalmatian coast and some islands host, appropriately, the Dalmatian ringlet (*Proterebia afra*).

below left The Hungarian glider is an elegant and boldly marked insect. (DP)
below right The Bulgarian ringlet is found only in Bulgaria. (EE)

The sombre goldenring *Cordulegaster bidentata* is one of the region's larger dragonflies. (MM)

DRAGONFLIES

Dragonflies (Odonata) are an increasingly popular group of insects amongst amateur naturalists. These winged wonders are able to hover, fly backwards, reach speeds of 50km per hour and then come to a sudden halt in mid-air. They are always found near wetlands as water is essential for them to complete their life cycle. Taxonomists have conveniently placed all of the world's species into two main groups: the true dragonflies (Anisoptera) and the damselflies (Zygoptera). When at rest the former hold their wings out from their body, forming a cross, whilst the latter close their wings above their body. The Anisoptera include hawkers (Aeshnidae), club-tailed dragonflies (Gomphidae), golden-ringed dragonflies (Cordulegastridae), emeralds (Corduliidae) and chasers, skimmers and darters (Libellulidae). The Zygoptera include demoiselles (Calopterygidae), emerald damselflies (Lestidae), white-legged damselflies (Platycnemididae) and red and blue damselflies (Coenagrionidae).

THE EYES HAVE IT!
Have you ever noticed how a dragonfly always spots you before you spot it? This is because dragonflies have incredibly good eyesight. A dragonfly eye can be composed of up to 30,000 individual lenses whereas a human eye has only one lens.

The big-eyed scrutiny of a moorland hawker *Aeshea juncea* (KP)

SPECIALITIES
Many central and eastern European countries have impressive national lists of Odonata – more than 70 species have been recorded in the Czech Republic, Slovakia and Croatia (compared with 38 in all Britain). Bulgaria is another dragonfly-rich country and home to regional specialities like the Bulgarian emerald (*Somatochlora borisi*), which was only discovered in 1999. Dragonfly-watching tours to Bulgaria regularly find 50 species in ten days. In addition to quantity, there is also quality, as several decidedly eastern species are restricted to this region. For example, the Siberian winter damsel (*Sympecma paedisca*), dark whiteface (*Leucorrhinia albifrons*) and lilypad whiteface (*L. caudalis*) are found in Poland and the Baltic States. The very localised bladetail (*Lindenia tetraphylla*) occurs on coastal wetlands in Croatia and Montenegro, and the Balkan emerald (*Somatochlora meridionalis*) and Balkan goldenring (*Cordulegaster heros*) are both found in pockets from Slovakia southwards to Serbia and Bulgaria. The latter is the largest dragonfly in all Europe, with females often over 9cm long.

below left Balkan emerald *Somatochlora meridionalis* (MM)
below right Balkan goldenring (DS)

ASSORTED CREEPY-CRAWLIES

In addition to the ever popular dragonflies and butterflies, the region is home to many other fascinating invertebrates (animals without backbones) of all shapes, sizes and colours. They are found just about everywhere, from the lowland grasslands of Hungary to the rocky tops of the Carpathian and Balkan ranges, munching their way through foliage or devouring each other. When on holiday children are often expert finders and observers of worms, leeches, snails, slugs, grasshoppers, crickets, mantises, shield bugs, cicadas, bees, wasps, ants, beetles and spiders.

The Carpathian blue slug (*Bielzia coerulans*) is arguably Europe's most attractive mollusc. For once the English name is entirely accurate; this slug is indeed a deep blue colour and lives in the Carpathian range and adjacent foothills. It is best sought just after rainfall when it comes out from the leaf litter and slithers across roads and paths.

top Ladybird spider *Eresus* sp (MM)
above Carpathian blue slug (FB)

The mole cricket (*Gryllotalpa gryllotalpa*) is a stocky, velvety-haired insect, with mole-like subterranean habits. For most of the year it is hard to see as it lives in burrows excavated with its spade-like forelegs. It is also rather nocturnal, though can be seen when it takes to the wing on summer evenings and also when males serenade females with a monotonous, low-pitched toad-like churring 'song'. Though on the verge of extinction in Britain, mole crickets are fairly common in the lowlands of central and eastern Europe.

The mole cricket is built for hard labour (MM)

The rosalia longicorn is a splendid long-horned beetle of mature beech forests. (Pavel Krásenský/Naturfoto)

There are hundreds of species of long-horned beetle (Cerambycidae) and their larvae are experts at nibbling into tree-bark and timber, a habit which does not endear them to foresters. In their adult stage many long-horned beetles are large, attractive insects, with males in particular sporting impressive long antennae. The beech forests of the region are home to the rosalia longicorn (*Rosalia alpina*), a handsome member of the family with its light blue body, legs and antennae all dotted with black. Though both sexes have long antennae those of males, at between 3–4cm long, are twice as long as their bodies.

121

The praying mantis (*Mantis religiosa*) is a fairly common assassin of grassy places throughout the southern, warmer countries of the region. It takes its name from its habit of holding its forelegs together as if in prayer, although 'preying mantis' would be as good a name as those same legs are used to seize passing insects. In lean times praying mantises are not averse to a bit of cannibalism, though the female does not always eat her partner after mating. At 6cm males are smaller than females, which reach 8cm. When threatened these elegant insects rear up, spread their limbs, fan out their wings, open their mouths and generally make themselves look as big and formidable as possible. When picking one up watch out for those pincer-like forearms which can grip a finger with surprising force.

Scorpions (order Scorpiones) are not insects but arachnids, as are spiders, ticks and mites. Insects have six legs, whilst arachnids have eight. Scorpions are viviparous (giving birth to live young) and the young, which are pale replicas of their mother, are carried on her back. Around 25 species of scorpions are found in Europe, mostly in the drier south. The Balkans hosts a good range of these often misunderstood invertebrates, including the rare *Euscorpius carpathicus*, found mainly in Romania, *E. gamma* which was only described in 2000 and inhabits the Adriatic countries, and *E. hadzii* which can be seen in gardens and orchards with old walls and sometimes enters houses. The yellow scorpion *Mesobuthus gibbosus* grows to 7.5cm in length and often appears rather translucent. It lives in bare, arid areas from the coast up into the mountains, by day typically hiding under rocks, logs and in crevices. Scorpions are nocturnal hunters, preying on other invertebrates which they grasp in their claws and then paralyse with a venomous sting from the famous tail. The stings of scorpions found in the region are relatively harmless to most people (said to be similar to those of wasps and bees), though they are painful and cause numbness. To be on the safe side, never handle any scorpion.

The yellow scorpion is a sizeable and impressive-looking beast. (TT)

LOOKING FOR WILDLIFE

Scoping the terrain (FB)

Birdwatching on Saaremaa, Estonia's largest island (MK)

There are many ways in which to seek out and enjoy the wildlife of eastern and central Europe. How much you see will depend partly upon your preparation – finding out where and when to go. But, wherever you go, you will get more from your trip by staying alert to the natural world and learning to interpret its clues.

FIELD CRAFT

When watching animals, try to move and think like one. Tread slowly and carefully, do not walk directly towards them, and avoid making eye contact – especially with larger mammals. Some mammals rely on their senses of smell and hearing, so keeping downwind can also help – as can feigning complete lack of interest. It is usually best to keep one's distance, in some cases for safety but mainly because most animals are easily spooked. Remember: binoculars are not only for distant views; you can also use them to scan the ground for resting butterflies and dragonflies.

A good torch is important at dawn and dusk. Many mammals are most active at these times, especially nocturnal ones, such as bats, mustelids and dormice, as are most owls. Earlier is better for most songbirds, while many amphibians prefer to go about their business when the sun is down. Once found, salamanders, newts and toads often stay put, trusting in their camouflage or toxic secretions to protect them. Frogs are more likely to leap towards safety at your approach.

Some animals are only active by day. Butterflies, dragonflies, lizards and snakes all need the sun to warm them up to operating temperature. Reptiles emerge to bask as the day progresses, but retreat into the shade during the hottest hours to avoid overheating. The best times to observe them are mid-morning or on overcast days. Snakes and salamanders often become active during, or just after, showers.

TRACKS AND SIGNS

Very few animals hang around when humans are present and wildlife walks can often end with little, if anything, of note observed. Sometimes it seems as if the countryside is deserted, but the animals are there, they may just be keeping their heads down. An observant eye, however, will spot all kinds of evidence of animal activity: tracks, trails, droppings, pellets, nests and feeding remains. A trained eye will find even more clues – dust baths, wallows, scent-marking posts – and match them to the animals responsible. Some of the evidence that animals leave does not require such a Sherlock Holmes-like approach: for example, molehills, anthills and beaver lodges are hard to miss.

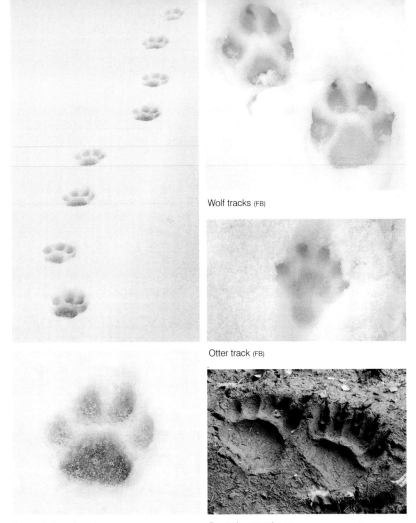

Wolf tracks (FB)

Otter track (FB)

top and above Lynx tracks (FB)

Brown bear tracks (TT)

Animal tracks are not easy to find unless they are made on soft surfaces such as mud, damp sand or snow. The best places to look for tracks include watercourses, beaches and also along manmade paths and roads, since mammals in particular will use these, especially when they cut conveniently through difficult terrain. The best times to search for tracks are after light rain or snowfall. Finding and identifying tracks is not easy and perfect prints are rare – too much rain washes them away and very fine sand or soft snow collapses and distorts their shape – but it is a rewarding way of finding out what wildlife is active in an area. Most animals follow established routes. They do not wander haphazardly about but rather tread a well-beaten network of paths. This means that not only do they leave tracks but also trails. Trails invariably follow the easiest line through the terrain, and obstacles such as boulders and tree stumps are usually circumnavigated. Repeated use results in trails becoming worn and obvious, eg: otter slides or vole tunnels under snow or thick grass.

Hoofing it

All the hoofed mammals in Europe have four toes but in most cases only the front two make a print as the two hind toes (dew claws) are small, placed high up the leg and seldom touch the ground. This results in a print of two clearly separated splayed or parallel slots, though roe deer and elk sometimes leave dew claw marks. Wild boar prints are composed of two large front slots and two clear points at the rear made by the dew claws, which always touch the ground. The widest part of the print is at the rear between the two dew claws. The hooves of European bison leave an imprint very much like those of large domestic cattle. In places where there is no domestic stock, like the heart of a Polish forest, such prints can only mean one thing.

Claws and paws

There is always more chance of finding a large predator track than actually seeing the animal itself. Finding a large paw print is always exciting and the thought that a wolf or lynx passed by recently brings out the tracker in all of us. The first things to note are size, shape, number of toes and presence or absence of claw marks. Canids show claw marks; cats, which retract their claws when moving, do not. Wolf prints are difficult to tell from those of large dogs, as both tend to leave imprints of four toes and four claws on each foot. The fifth toe is found only on the two front feet and does not leave an imprint as it does not touch the ground. Wolf claw marks are longer and sharper than those of domestic dogs. Fox and jackal prints are also hard to tell from domestic dogs, since the various breeds all have different paw sizes. Lynx prints are three times bigger than the average tabby's, and this is the easiest way to rule out a domestic cat – though wildcat prints are very difficult to separate from those of the latter. Most brown bear prints are obvious, showing five large toe pads and long claw marks on each foot. The forepaw prints are shorter and broader than the rear ones. Mature males' prints are up to 28cm long and 20cm wide. Smaller bear prints recall those that bare-footed humans leave on the beach, except that the innermost toe on a bear foot is very small, whereas on a human it's the biggest toe. A whole range of smaller mammals leave footprints, not to mention reptiles and amphibians, but many of these are difficult to assign to species.

Body prints

Some animals are unable to leave paw or footprints as they lack feet. Seals leave a very characteristic broad trail on wet beaches where they have dragged themselves along. Parallel flipper prints with five claw marks each lie either side of the trail. Snakes make two kinds of trail: those that move in a winding motion leave a series of ripples, roughly S-shaped, where sections of their bodies have touched soft ground, whilst large snakes move forward in a straighter line and leave a wider, single track marked with scale imprints.

HOME COMFORTS

Many animals use a long-term dwelling of some kind, most commonly as a place to rear their young. Whether this home makes use of natural features or is built from scratch, many are distinctive and finding one may afford the opportunity to see the occupant.

Grey partridges will dig themselves into snow to forage, keep warm and escape predators. (MV)

Holes

Several mammal species live in holes, which they either excavate themselves or usurp. Some, like sousliks, live in communal burrow systems, whilst others, such as hamsters, live in individual burrows. All hole-dwellers benefit from the greater security and cosier climate of a cavity. Note the size of the entrance, as this corresponds to the size of the mammal that uses it. Tracks and droppings by the hole suggest the hole is in use. Once you have identified the creator of a hole, remember that another animal may be using it. For example, polecats take over souslik burrows and snakes will occupy holes made by small rodents.

Nests

Hedgehogs, dormice, mice, squirrels and, of course, many birds, build nests. When trying to determine who made what, location, size and shape should be noted. Most birds build open, cupped nests, though some, like the wren and penduline tit, weave nests with a single hole or spout entrance. Some birds do not make nests at all but rely on others to do the work for them. For example, magpies are busy nest builders whose work benefits small falcons and long-eared owls, whilst large raptor nests may be used by saker falcons or larger owls. Autumn and winter, when there is less foliage on trees, are the best seasons for spotting nests, even though they may not be in use. Never approach too close and disturb a sitting bird.

This black woodpecker's industry may later benefit other animals. (DT)

WOODPECKER HOLES

Woodpeckers excavate their own nest-holes in trees. Most woodpeckers hack out several cavities a year, mostly in spring, and use some as nesting sites and others as roosts. All kinds of woodland wildlife benefit from this carpentry: flycatchers, owls, dormice, martens, hornets and bees all use woodpecker holes.

top left The common tern's nest is little more than a scrape. (FB)
top right Disused magpie nests often provide a home for owls and birds of prey (SS)
above left Little grebes nest among marshy vegetation. (FB)
above right Penduline tits build an elaborate, sock-shaped nest. (FB)

DROPPINGS

Droppings are a common indication of the presence of wildlife. White splashes on cliffs can betray the nests or roosts of birds which would otherwise be too high up to spot and, if were it not for piles of droppings in caves or buildings, bat roosts would often go unnoticed. When in search of wildlife, animal excrement should be actively sought out. Enthusiasts will note the size, shape, colour, contents, odour and location of any droppings stumbled upon. Texture is an important clue: dry, hard droppings mean some time has passed since they were deposited; moist or runny droppings indicate they are fresh and that the responsible animal may be nearby. Droppings come in a great variety of shapes: straight, coiled, twisted, oval, rounded or sausage-shaped. European bison dung often resembles a pile of burnt chocolate pancakes. As a rule herbivores produce lots of neat round or oval droppings, whilst carnivores produce long, cylindrical ones that taper to a point. Some animals leave piles of droppings (wild boar, deer, brown bear), others hide them (lynx) or use latrines (badger) whilst others just scatter them around at random.

Many animals deposit their droppings in prominent places, using them to mark territory borders. Wolf scat can often be found at trail junctions, whilst minks and beech martens place theirs on the top of stones, stumps, logs and tussocks. Droppings can be poked with a stick and broken up to see if there are any obvious contents. Bones, skulls, chitin, feathers, fur and fruit stones all identify what an animal has been eating and sometimes can even indicate the exact species responsible for the dropping. Diet influences colour and texture: animals that have consumed berries will produce bluish, reddish or purplish droppings, whereas those that have eaten bones will drop white ones. There are also seasonal differences: in winter elk droppings look like piles of chipolatas, whilst in summer wet dung is dropped. Bird droppings are often rather watery and hence more temporary, though there are exceptions: grouse droppings are fairly solid and resemble catkins or cigarette butts.

Pellets

Predatory birds regurgitate as pellets food that they cannot digest. Birds of prey, herons, storks, crows, gulls and, of course, owls, all cough up these neat little parcels which, like mammal droppings, contain food remains. Different species produce different kinds of pellet, with size, shape and contents all significant. Pellets often accumulate below night-time roosts and, where communal roosts are involved such as with long-eared owls in winter, pellets pile up into large mounds.

Otter spraints contain telltale remains of crabs and crayfish. (FB)

GETTING OUT AND ABOUT

Eastern and central Europe is not Africa: you won't find the animals by simply sitting in a minibus. To get the most from the region you need to step out and explore. But this doesn't necessarily mean long hikes into the wilderness: there are many ways, and many places, in which to discover wildlife.

BOAT TRIPS

Some marine animals can be observed from land, and in the case of seals actually on it, but boat trips are the only way to search for cetaceans, and are often the best way of viewing offshore bird colonies. The wildlife of the Adriatic and Baltic seas can be seen by taking scheduled ferries, though passengers will not be able to influence the route to encompass anything special that is spotted. Boat and ferry trips are also subject to, and at the mercy of, the weather, so waterproofs and warm layers of clothing should be taken along. Occasionally an cast-iron stomach may be needed, too.

Croatia's archipelago can only really be experienced by boat. Ferries ply between the major islands and, in summer, excursion craft work the smaller islands. Dolphins will sometimes follow such boats. Seabirds and Eleonora's falcons can be seen on journeys around the rocky islands of the Kornati archipelago and Vis Island. Boat trips to and around Estonia's islands can be a good way of seeing grey seals and, in spring and autumn, masses of migrating waterfowl.

Boat trips on freshwater wetlands can be frustrating for naturalists and are often unnecessary, as much the same wildlife can be seen from the land. An exception to this is the Danube Delta in Romania, which should be experienced by cruising around it. Boat trips out of Tulcea, the gateway into the delta, are offered by local companies. The best trips include overnight accommodation on 'house-boats', which have open upper-decks suitable for tripods and telescopes.

White storks find ideal nest sites on manmade structures. (MV)

AROUND TOWN

Food draws animals into urban habitats. Most urban areas in the region back onto countryside, and animals find settlements convenient places to scrounge food. Urban rubbish tips, hotel refuse bins and gardens are all places where easy meals can be found, particularly in harsh winters. Many of central and eastern Europe's towns and cities are havens for wildlife. Some of the region's capital cites even have decent tracts of forest right on their doorsteps and deer, wild boar and who knows what else may pop into town.

Some animals no longer even bother to commute, having colonised urban areas and become permanent residents. A classic example is the beech marten, a night-time reveiler that keeps a low profile but which is actually common. This mustelid sleeps in attics, garages and under car bonnets, and is infamous as a nibbler of electric cables. Some bats now depend almost entirely upon buildings for roost and nursery sites and are rare away from settlements.

Where rivers and canals flow through urban areas, they serve as corridors along which animals travel. For example, beavers can be seen within the city limits of Vilnius and Warsaw. In parts of the Carpathians brown bears visit gardens and orchards in villages that adjoin forests, and winter-sports resorts also see bears drawn to hotel rubbish bins. In Romania brown bears regularly come out from the forest and, with their cubs in tow, openly raid skips around towns such as Brasov and Sinaia. Wolves have also been seen entering and leaving Brasov, though when doing so they keep a much lower profile than bears. Such urban wolves pose no threat at all to people, unlike brown bears which, despite being apparently placid and 'urbanised', are unpredictable animals which should never be approached (see Mammals chapter).

GUIDED TRIPS

With so many great destinations, and so much to see, an increasing number of tour operators are running guided wildlife holidays in the region. Group travel is not for everyone, but there are advantages in joining an organised tour. Groups contain more pairs of eyes, which usually means more wildlife is spotted and most group travellers are happy to share what they find with other participants.

A group tour might (but not necessarily) cost more than a do-it-yourself trip, but this is offset by better use of time and having local expertise at hand. Most tours will have a local driver who will get the group straight to the best wildlife sites (rather than wasting time deciphering road signs and possibly getting lost) and a wildlife guide. A local naturalist guide will be able to take you directly to the habitats, and sometimes the exact territories, of the species you want to observe and provide instant and invaluable insights into wildlife occurrence and behaviour. Local guides can often be hired by the day, which may suit individuals and families travelling independently, and can usually be found via the internet.

Some tour operators are better than others, and a glossy brochure or a high-tech website does not always mean that a company is experienced. Try to find a company that suits your style of wildlife-watching. Before booking a tour ask questions and establish the following:

• Has the company been to a particular destination before?
• Will there be an experienced guide? (Ask whether local experts will be involved.)
• How big is the group? (10–12 is probably optimal, more than 16 is pushing it.)
• What is the pace of the tour? (Will it be strenuous or easy-going, focused on ticking off species or will there be time to study what is found?)
• Is it suitable for photographers? (Photographic tours are not for all.)
• Does the company operate responsibly and support local conservation?

PHOTOGRAPHY

Wildlife photography is no longer the exclusive preserve of professionals. More and more people are out there with cameras, on their knees getting shots of butterflies or holed up in hides waiting for that large carnivore to appear. The digital age has made photography less expensive and less painful but taking pictures of wildlife in central and eastern Europe is rarely as easy as on, for example, an African safari. Not only are most of the animals smaller, but they are also often a bit more dubious about tourists pointing huge lenses in their direction. The same skills will, however, be necessary and the same rules will apply. You will need a long lens, perhaps a zoom, a wide-angle lens for those panoramic compositions and a macro lens for the insects.

A camouflaged hide is for the serious photographer. (FB)

PHOTOGRAPHER'S TIPS

- Vehicles make great mobile hides. The human form is concealed and many animals allow a much closer approach. With practice a car can be discreetly manoeuvred to follow the movements of a subject.
- Think about lighting. Once a subject has been found, light conditions will largely dictate whether things go well or not.
- Use a bean bag. Forget those expensive and heavy window clamps.
- Don't forget: spare films, batteries, charger for digital camera, lenses, filters, cleaning cloths, tripod, beanbag, a waterproof bag that holds everything and any instruction booklets.
- Use your field skills: be patient, take your time, allow wildlife to settle, try not to make eye contact, keep still, avoid sudden movements and stay silent.
- Follow regulations: always check reserve and national park rules on photography.

Wildlife walks are for everyone! (AB)

Soomaa National Park, Estonia: you may need a boat in spring; snowshoes in winter. (AA)

PLANNING YOUR TRIP

When planning a wildlife-watching holiday, first decide what you want to see. Is it going to be a birding trip? Is seeing 'eastern' butterflies or large mammals the objective? Will you want to take photographs, draw or paint or just observe species? Perhaps you are an all-round naturalist and are happy to watch anything that runs, crawls, flies or swims your way. If you are travelling as a family or in a group then there may well be a range of interests and priorities.

Unrealistic objectives and targets should be avoided: it's unlikely you will be able to visit all the key sites or succeed in observing everything on your 'wish-list'. It is often a good idea to concentrate on two or three specific places rather than tearing around cramming in as many reserves as possible. Combine different habitats, landscapes and elevations: perhaps a few days on the coast and around lowland wetlands, followed by time in an upland forest. If your trip is mainly for other reasons than watching wildlife – business or a family holiday – then do a bit of homework, reading up on the area you are to visit and the wildlife you might be able to sneak off and see whilst there.

WHEN TO GO

Timing is crucial. If you have a choice, choose the optimum period for the wildlife that most interests you. It's probably best to avoid winter, as most of central and eastern Europe sees sub-zero temperatures and plenty of ice and snow. Besides the absence of avian summer visitors, butterflies, dragonflies and hibernating species, winter also means shorter days and more difficult driving conditions. On the other hand, winter is often the perfect season for tracking large mammals like wolves and lynx and November to March is the time to see flocks of red-breasted geese in Romania and Bulgaria.

The Low Tatras in Slovakia are, in fact, rather high. (FB)

The first marmots, sousliks, hamsters, dormice, reptiles and amphibians appear in March and April. Early butterflies take to the wing in April and May, but most wait until June and July. September is the traditional month to hear the bellowing of rutting red deer stags. By November most of the animals that hibernate are already tucked up somewhere warm. Interesting birds can be seen year-round but, of course, there are specific periods for specific species. Forest owls call mostly early in the year. Some white storks return to their nests as early as March, shorebirds pour north in April and early May, returning south from July to September, and common crane numbers in Hungary peak in October. Overall, May is probably the best birding month as breeding is in full swing across the region.

WHAT TO TAKE

It is not so much what should be taken on a wildlife trip but what should be left at home. Size and weight will certainly influence what is packed for those taking flights. Keener birders will carry a telescope and tripod, lepidopterists may pack a butterfly net, usually a handy fold-up model (always make sure locally that using a net is allowed and never 'collect' butterflies) and photographers will invariably be overloaded. You'll need a range of clothing, which will largely depend upon the season (best to check the local weather online in the days prior to departure) but also on elevation. You might need a sun hat on the coast one day and a woolly one in the mountains the next. In general think layers, items that can be put on or taken off according to changes in temperature, and avoid bright colours.

Grasslands in Dobrudja, Romania, are rich in flowers in spring. (DP)

The High Fatras in Slovakia (FB)

Other things to take are:
- Field guides: choose those that cover the entire European continent to ensure that central and eastern European species are included. Identification guides to birds, bats, reptiles and amphibians, butterflies and dragonflies are now available (see *Further Information*) but weight will surely mean that some stay at home.
- Notebook: to make notes and sketches of your observations. Don't forget a supply of pens and pencils. Keep in a waterproof pouch or plastic bag.
- Maps: most national parks and reserves have detailed maps, though they may be hard to obtain in advance. Maps should be used together with a compass or a portable GPS.
- Binoculars: essential for all wildlife-watchers. Take a pair best suited to your objectives: 10x50 or 8x40 for birdwatching and general wildlife-watching; a compact pair with fine close-focusing for insects.
- Camera: be sure to pack all the accessories, cables, lens cleaning materials and spare batteries and memory cards/films.

- Tripod: along with any necessary adapters for cameras and telescopes.
- Accessories: sunblock, sunglasses, insect repellent, water-bottle, Thermos flask, small first-aid kit, Swiss army knife, plastic bags to keep things dry and to store collected items like pellets, a compact, waterproof backpack to carry everything in.

Flood at the Lemmejõgi River, Estonia (AA)

View from Julian Alps to Savinjake Alps in Slovenia (AB)

HEALTH AND SAFETY

It may be a cliché but it's true: prevention is better than cure. Another well-worn slogan should not be scoffed at either: be prepared. Always consult the travel guides (or check online) as to your destination's health regulations, recommendations and any recent scares.

- Medicines: take sufficient supplies of any personal medicines. They may not be available locally and, even if they are, language and/or local regulations may mean they are hard to obtain.
- Inoculations: have any necessary jabs well before you travel.
- Dehydration: always drink plenty of water and carry a supply when away from settlements. Mineral water is widely available and inexpensive throughout the region.
- Ticks: in some areas ticks may carry diseases like meningoencephalitis. Before walking in deciduous woodlands or grasslands spray around the ankles, cuffs and collar with insect repellent. Wear shoes rather than sandals, a long-sleeved shirt and trousers rather than shorts. Check clothing soon after leaving a potential tick area and simply flick any of the beasts off before they crawl under your clothing. A precautionary jab against meningoencephalitis is available. Gently remove any embedded ticks with fine tweezers or a 'Tick Twister' tool.
- Snakebites: in the unlikely event that a viper sinks its fangs into you, don't panic, lie down, avoid all food and drink except water. Do not apply a tourniquet and never try to suck out the venom. Seek medical attention as soon as possible. Prevention measures include wearing closed footwear, keeping to footpaths and using common sense – see *Reptiles* chapter for more.
- Brown bears: the majority of bears avoid people, but all are potentially dangerous (see *Mammals* chapter).
- Driving: central and eastern Europe has some of the continent's most creative drivers. Though the rules are the same everywhere most countries have their unique ways of interpreting them. Adhering to the 'If you can't beat 'em, join 'em' approach is often prudent. In rural areas allow for horse-drawn traffic and in the north keep an eye open for elk.

WHERE TO GO

Lake Alepu, Bulgaria (EE)

BOSNIA & HERZEGOVINA

One of Europe's newest countries, Bosnia & Herzegovina covers just over 51,000km², with a population of around 4.5 million. Croatia lies to the west and north, Serbia to the east and Montenegro to the southeast. If it were not for 20km of Adriatic coastline, north of Dubrovnik, the country would be totally land-locked.

This is a mountainous country and has almost 50% forest cover, including virgin stands of beech and conifer. There are many rolling hill ranges, gorges and, at the highest elevations, alpine-like meadows and pastures. Lowland landscapes in the north and southwest are typified by arable land, often worked in a traditional manner, with plenty of edge habitats and *polje* (lowland depressions prone to flooding). In the northeast there are marshes and wooded floodplains along the River Sava where it forms the border with Croatia and Serbia. There are still some security and safety issues in the country, including the risk of unexploded mines in a handful of localities (less than 4% of land area is affected) but adventurous travellers might make a few wildlife discoveries.

This country has two national parks, both in the uplands. **Sutjeska** (175km²) nestles on the border with Montenegro. This is a wild area, with mixed forests, rushing rivers, waterfalls and the country's highest peak, Maglić (2,386m). The park's centrepiece is a magnificent old-growth beech, fir, spruce and black pine forest at Perucica. Brown bears and wolves are here, and forest birds include white-backed woodpeckers (of the southern *lilfordi* race) and three-toed woodpeckers (*alpinus* race). **Kozara** lies in the north, in Krajina. Part of the Dinaric range, its

Maglić Mountain: the highest peak in Bosnia (TC)

rolling karstic peaks are shrouded in dense mixed forests and hold a good mix of forest wildlife, but there are no large carnivores here as hunting seems to take priority over conservation.

Hutova Blato is a karst wetland reserve in the southwest. The Neretva river lies just to the north, before it flows into Croatia and the Adriatic. Pygmy cormorants and ferruginous ducks breed and other wetland birds stop over in large numbers, particularly in autumn. In summer this is a superb place for dragonflies and amphibians.

Bosnia & Herzegovina has several Balkan specialities. Reptiles to look out for include Dalmatian algyroides, Balkan green lizard, Dalmatian wall lizard, Mosor rock and sharp-snouted rock lizards, and Balkan, Dahl's and large whip snakes, while notable amphibians include Alpine and fire salamanders, Balkan crested newt and Balkan stream frog. Localised insect species are numerous and include butterflies such as Balkan green-veined white, Balkan clouded yellow, Balkan fritillary, Ottoman brassy ringlet and black ringlet, while the impressive tally of at least 50 dragonfly species includes sombre goldenring.

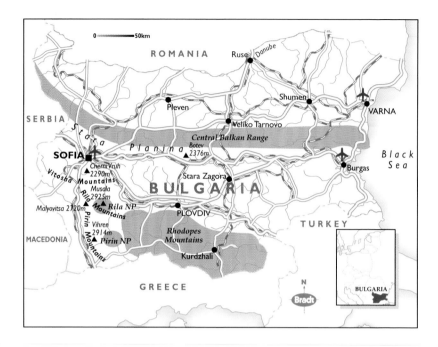

BULGARIA

Covering almost 111,000km², Bulgaria borders Romania to the north, Macedonia and Serbia to the west, Greece to the south and Turkey to the southeast. In the east is 354km of Black Sea coastline. The population is less than 7.4 million.

Bulgaria has a combination of temperate and Mediterranean climates and a range of upland, lowland and marine habitats, which results in a very varied fauna. There's a landscape for everybody: craggy peaks, alpine pastures, gorges, old-growth forests, dry scrub, stony steppe, marshes, lagoons, dunes and sea. The border with Romania is dominated by the Danube, which is lined with riverine woods and manmade fishponds. Much of the country's farmland is worked non-intensively.

The country is internationally important for brown bears and marbled polecats, golden jackals are quite common and there's a Balkan race of chamois. The most likely cetacean to be seen is the harbour porpoise. Birds include several breeding species which are very rare further west, such as paddyfield warbler, pied wheatear and semi-collared flycatcher. Large flocks of red-breasted geese winter on the coast, and the Via Pontica flyway sees flocks of pelicans, raptors and up to 250,000 white storks every August and September.

Bulgaria is superb for 'herps'. Hermann's and spur-thighed tortoises, Kotschy's gecko, meadow lizard, four-lined snake and nose-horned viper are all fairly widespread. In the south, Balkan terrapin, sand boa and Dahl's and large whip snakes are possible. The Balkan crested newt is in one of its global strongholds and both spadefoots occur, eastern spadefoot being more widespread. On the invertebrate front, there are over 200 species of butterfly, including the endemic

Cape Kaliakra (Nos Kaliakra): a headland on Bulgaria's Black Sea coast (NP)

Bulgarian ringlet. The 60 species of dragonfly found here include Bulgarian emerald, Balkan emerald and Balkan goldenring.

The country has three national parks, Pirin, Rila and Stara Planina, all of which are uplands. **Rila** is the largest and includes Musala (2,925m), the country's highest peak. There are a few wolves and brown bears here as well as the most chamois in Bulgaria. Birds include wallcreeper, Alpine accentor and Alpine chough, while reptiles include Erhard's wall lizard. In summer high meadows are alive with butterflies, specialities being Bulgarian and black ringlets and Balkan fritillary. **Pirin** has similar landscapes and wildlife, though lepidopterists will be keen to find the near-endemic butterflies such as Gavarnie, Phalakron and Higgin's anomalous blues.

About 75km north of Varna is the coastal headland of **Nos Kaliakra** where the dry steppe hosts European souslik, Romanian hamster and marbled polecat, Hermann's and spur-thighed tortoises and eastern spadefoot. Black-headed bunting and four species of wheatear breed. Flocks of rose-coloured starlings invade and nest most summers.

CROATIA

Croatia is sparsely populated (under 4.5 million in 56,542km²). The country is a crescent shape, with Slovenia to the northwest, Hungary to the north, Serbia to the east, Bosnia-Herzegovina to the east and south and Montenegro to the south. The west is dominated by 1,777km of Adriatic coast and over 1,000 offshore islands, which add a further 4,058km of shoreline.

Inland Croatia has lake-dotted forested uplands and, in the northeast, a fertile plain with marshes, fish farms and arable land lies by the Danube and Drava rivers. The Dinaric Alps run from the northwest to southeast. Large areas of maquis and karst terrain lie just off the rocky Dalmatian coastline. Only 66 of Croatia's islands are inhabited and just 20 heavily touristed, and it is this 'seascape' that sets Croatia apart from all other countries in the region. The islands and coast have typical Mediterranean landscapes of grazed pastures, sea-blasted scrub and citrus groves. In Dalmatia the climate is mild all year round, but watch out for the *bura*, a chilly wind that blows in from the northeast.

Mammals include brown bear, wolf and lynx in remote areas, as well as numerous bats in karst areas. Bottle-nosed dolphins swim in the Adriatic (the Blue

Aerial view of the Brijuni Islands (Mark Edward Smith/Tips)

World Dolphin Research Centre on Veli Losinj is worth visiting). Key birds are rock partridge, Eleonora's falcon, Audouin's gull and eastern orphean warbler.

Croatia is superb for reptiles, with highlights such as Dalmatian algyroides, Horvath's and Mosor rock lizards, Dalmatian wall lizard, European glass lizard, Balkan whip snake, leopard and cat snakes and nose-horned viper.

Amphibians include fire salamander, Italian crested and Danube crested newts, and olms inhabit underground caves at **Krka** and **Ogulin**, though visiting is not permitted. Karst regions like **Paklenica** host 80 species of butterfly with little tiger blue, blue argus, anomalous blue, Balkan marbled white and Dalmatian ringlet amongst the specialities. There are over 70 regular dragonfly species: areas such as the **Neretva Delta**, **Lonjsko polje** and **Kopacki rit** host at least 40 species each and the larger islands are home to over 30 species. Highlights include bladetail, ornate bluet and Balkan emerald.

There are eight well-organised national parks in Croatia. The scenic **Plitvice** is the most famous but often packed with visitors. **Risnjak** is a limestone range on the Slovenian border, with brown bear, lynx, owls and woodpeckers. **Sjeverni Velebit** is a similarly rugged upland. The limestone gorges at **Paklenica** are excellent for birds, butterflies and reptiles. **Krka's** karst landscapes (waterfalls, lakes, gorges) lie along the rushing River Krka. **Kornati** protects marine habitats and 101 islands and islets, mostly uninhabited and covered in maquis, karst fields, citrus groves and abandoned pastures. Dolphins are possible on boat trips here and around the Brijuni Islands. The rare Audouin's gull nests on islets off **Mljet**.

At 66km long, **Cres** is the Adriatic's second largest island. It has a rugged coastline of cliffs, pebble beaches and rocky inlets. Inland there is stony scrub, olive groves and hornbeam, chestnut and pinewoods. Cres's main attraction is a colony of griffon vultures on sea-cliffs near Beli.

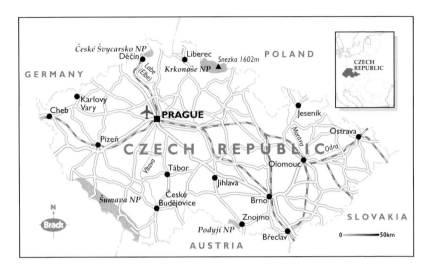

CZECH REPUBLIC

Totally landlocked, the Czech Republic borders Austria to the south, Germany to the west and north, Poland to the north and Slovakia to the east. The population is around ten million. The vast majority of visitors to the country never leave Prague and are probably unaware of the natural heritage of the country's 78,866km².

The varied topography of the Czech Republic means diverse habitats, everything from bare alpine-like peaks down to lush lowland grasslands. There are large tracts

Rozmberk fishpond is the largest 'pond' in the country. (Jan Sevčík/Naturfoto)

of forest: dwarf pine in the high mountains, mixed old-growth, gallery woods, parkland and plantations. Natural and manmade wetlands such as tarns, upland and lowland peatbogs and mires, oxbows, floodplains, lakes and reservoirs dot the country. In South Moravia open and wooded karst regions are key wildlife areas.

Lynx and beaver are increasing and there are healthy numbers of otter and 25 species of bat. A good blend of boreal and Mediterranean bird species includes all ten European woodpecker species. The country is a little too far north for many reptiles (the best areas to search are in South Moravia). Amphibians include fire salamander, yellow-bellied and fire-bellied toads and Alpine and Carpathian newts. In southern Moravia Danube and Italian crested newts are both at the very northern edge of their European ranges.

Several species of butterfly reach the northern and western edges of their European ranges here. Specialities are Danube clouded yellow, dusky large blue, damon blue and Sudeten ringlet. Dragonflies number some 70 species and particularly good places to look are the bogs and damp forests of the higher mountains, manmade fishponds and channels in south Bohemia, and ditches and wet woods in South Moravia. Ô175

There are four national parks in the country: **České Švycarsko**, **Krkonoše**, **Šumava** are forested, bog-dotted uplands and **Podyjí** a region of hills and valleys along the meandering River Dyje. **Šumava** lies along the German and Austrian borders and is mostly blanketed in spruce forests, peat-bogs and cut through by the Vltava river. There are some remnants of old-growth beech–fir–spruce forest, such as on Mount Boubin. Red and roe deer are abundant and lynx are doing well. Resident birds include Tengmalm's and pygmy owls, white-backed and three-toed woodpeckers and black and hazel grouse.

The **Dolní Morava Biosphere Reserve**, 35km south of Brno, is a mosaic of limestone hills, forests, steppe and wetlands. It is home to over 70 butterfly species and the most important place in the country for bats (22 species recorded). Resident birds include eagle owl and Syrian, black and grey-headed woodpeckers. Wallcreepers winter, as do large numbers of wildfowl on adjacent reservoirs.

Summer is a good time for dragonflies in the upland bogs of the Czech Republic. (Jan Sevčík/Naturfoto)

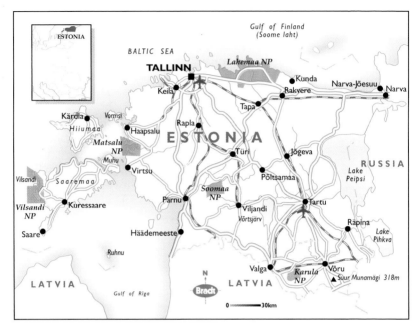

ESTONIA

Estonia is the northernmost Baltic state, with Latvia to the south and Russia to the east. The vast Lake Peipsi dominates the border with Russia. There is 3,794km of coast (2,540km on islands) with the Baltic and Riga Bay in the west and the Bay of Finland in the north. Covering just over 45,000km² and with a mere 1.4 million locals, there are plenty of remote spots in which to search for wildlife.

Estonia can be split into three basic zones: coast, islands and the interior. The northern coastline is rugged, with boulders, pebble shores, cliffs, inlets and peninsulas. The west coast is more gentle, with sandy beaches and dunes. Estonia has around 1,500 islands; the largest, Saaremaa, is 2,700km². Inland Estonia is flat and decidedly damp. At times it seems that the country is one great forested and sphagnum-moss-covered bog but in fact over 50% of Estonia is covered in trees, mainly spruce, pine and birch, and there are some old-growth stands. The right to roam, which Estonians call 'the everyman access principle', is taken very seriously.

Beavers and elk are common, there are some brown bear, wolf and lynx, and a few flying squirrels hang on, too. There are European mink on Hiiumaa and some islands host grey seals. Special birds include greater spotted eagle, great snipe, citrine wagtail, greenish warbler and parrot crossbill, all of which tempt western birders. Other birding highlights are masses of passage seabirds, wildfowl and waders and offshore winter rafts of Steller's eider.

Estonia is too far north for many reptiles, though there are sand and viviparous lizards, grass snake and adder.

Amphibians number just 11 species, including natterjack toad and moor, marsh, pool and edible frogs.

There are around 111 regular species of butterfly, including the likes of moorland clouded yellow, cranberry blue, bog fritillary, Lapland ringlet and Baltic grayling. Over 50 dragonfly species have been found in the country's nutrient-rich bogs, fens and brackish wetlands, highlights being Siberian winter damsel, dark bluet and Baltic hawkers.

The most remote of Estonia's five national parks is **Vilsandi**, founded to protect marine habitats, including ancient reefs, off the western shore of Saaremaa. Grey seals rest here and masses of seabirds and waterfowl pass through. There is a visitor centre at Loona on Saaremaa. **Matsalu** is a large, shallow bay with rocky and grassy shores, mudflats, saltmarsh, pastures, reedbeds, arable land and woods on the Baltic coast. Around 300 bird species have been recorded. There is a visitor centre at Penijõe. **Soomaa** is as Estonian as it gets, being 370km² of bog wilderness with naturally flooding rivers, home to brown bear, wolf, elk and a few flying squirrels. Breeding birds include black and hazel grouse, common crane, great snipe, wood sandpiper, Ural owl and three-toed woodpecker. There is a visitor centre at Kõrtsi-Tõramaa. In the south, **Karula** has some rolling hilly landscapes and forests, pastures, meadows and fens. Beavers, black storks, corncrakes and common spadefoots are fairly common. **Lahemaa** protects coastal and hinterland habitats on the Bay of Finland. There are few sandy shores in this area, instead rather desolate, rock-strewn coastlines. Inland forests are home to brown bear, wolf and lynx. There is a visitor centre in Palmse.

The **Luitemaa Nature Reserve** lies on the coast south of Pärnu and is a superb birdwatching area with marked trails, observation towers and a visitor centre at Pulgoja. There are coastal meadows, pastures, hayfields, dunes, pinewoods, sand flats and rocky islets. Spotted crake, penduline tit and nightjar breed. On passage masses of wildfowl, waders and terns pass this way. Natterjack toad is common.

Typical Estonian bogland: bring your wellingtons. (Focus Database/Tips)

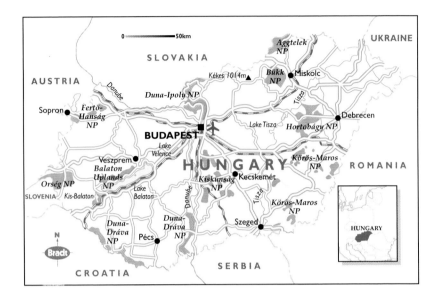

HUNGARY

Landlocked Hungary sits in the Carpathian Basin and is bordered by seven countries: Austria to the west, Slovakia to the north, Ukraine to the northeast, Romania to the east, Serbia and Croatia to the south and Slovenia to the southwest. Around ten million people live in its 93,000km², a fifth of them in Budapest.

Much of Hungary is flat, with extensive farmland and lowland grasslands, called *puszta*. This steppe-like habitat, which can be dry, wet or lightly wooded, is grazed by livestock and dotted with farmsteads and fish farms. The largest expanses lie on the Great Plain, east of the Danube. There are some forested (mainly deciduous) hill ranges, but no real mountains (only one peak tops 1,000m). If time is short the *puszta* and its wildlife should be the focus of any visit.

Hungary lacks large carnivores, though it is an important place for European sousliks and otters. Roe deer and wild boar are abundant. Bats include Geoffroy's, Bechstein's, greater and lesser mouse-eareds, greater noctule, serotine and pond bat. On the bird front, an important population of about 1,200 great bustards, the largest in Europe outside Iberia and Russia, resides here, mostly east of the Danube. Other highlights are saker falcon, eastern imperial eagle and aquatic warbler.

Hungary's reptiles include European pond terrapin, green and Balkan wall lizards and the endangered meadow viper. Common amphibians are fire-bellied and green toads, marsh, pool and edible frogs and Eurasian tree frog, with fire salamander and yellow-bellied toad localised in the uplands.

Butterflies number around 160 species with Hungarian glider, purple emperor, and plenty of skippers, whites, yellows, coppers, hairstreaks, blues, fritillaries and heaths to keep the experts busy. Over 60 species of dragonfly are found, with good areas being alkaline lakes in the Kiskunság region and the Hanság on the Austrian border. River clubtail is fairly common along the Danube, Tisza and other rivers.

Autumn sees masses of common cranes pass through eastern Hungary. (CF)

Hungary has ten national parks. **Aggtelek** (240km northeast of Budapest) is a karst area, excellent for birds, butterflies and around 25 species of bat. The **Bükk Hills** have similar wildlife but are higher and more forested. The rolling landscapes of the **Orség** nestle on the Austrian border and are important for butterflies like the scarce large blue. **Balaton-Uplands** is composed of several separate areas, wetlands, forests and grassland just above the summer playground of Lake Balaton. **Duna-Ipoly** is a collection of mainly upland habitats around the Danube Bend. Riverine habitats along the Croatian border are the main attraction of **Duna-Dráva**. About 200km east of Budapest, the **Hortobágy** is a lowland mosaic of grasslands and wetlands. Egrets, herons, marsh terns, red-footed and saker falcons and aquatic warbler all breed, and in autumn up to 100,000 common cranes stop over. Amphibians abound, too. The grasslands of the **Kiskunság** and **Körös-Maros** parks are home to lesser mole-rat, European souslik and great bustard. The core of **Fertö-Hanság**, on the Austrian border, is a shallow, saline lake fringed by vast reedbeds and grazing marshes. Masses of birds breed and stop here on migration.

The reedbeds and open water of **Lake Velence** are just 50km southwest of Budapest. Lots of herons, wildfowl, marsh terns, bluethroat and warblers breed. In autumn goose flocks roost here. It is excellent for pond terrapins, amphibians and dragonflies, too.

KALININGRAD

Kaliningrad is a small Russian enclave of 15,100km² on the Baltic, sandwiched between Lithuania to the north and Poland to the south. Around 80% of Kaliningrad's population of under one million live in urban areas, so once in the countryside there is usually little to disturb the wildlife-watcher.

With its boggy lowlands, gentle farmland and rural settlements, often with rooftop white stork nests, inland Kaliningrad is typically Baltic. Natural and planted forests cover about 25% of the enclave, mostly pine, spruce, birch and oak, but any traveller to this 'off the beaten track' destination should really head for Kaliningrad's 140km of coast and certainly visit the remarkable Curonian Spit. This strip of land that separates the Curonian Lagoon from the Baltic is the landscape feature that dominates Kaliningrad. Around 46km of the spit's total length of 98km lies in Kaliningrad, the rest in Lithuania. Outside the short sun-seeker season, the spit is a mysterious and ethereal place of pinewoods, beaches and drifting sand dunes, many over 30m high and some reaching 60m, that are under constant assault by waves and winds from the west. When the tide retreats this is a great place to beachcomb for animal tracks.

Elk, otter and beaver are fairly common and grey seals are occasionally seen offshore. In spring and autumn the Curonian spit is a major flyway for migrating birds of all kinds.

Kaliningrad is not rich in reptiles, though the sand and viviparous lizards, slow worm, smooth and grass snakes and adder occur. Amphibians include the common spadefoot and natterjack and green toads are fairly common.

Several typically northern, southern and eastern species of butterfly meet and overlap in range here and Kaliningrad lies in a zone where several dragonflies reach the northern limit of their European ranges. There are still things to learn about dragonflies in Kaliningrad, though presumably the same species occur as in neighbouring Poland and Lithuania.

The **Curonian Spit National Park** covers around 66km² and is a UNESCO World Heritage Site. It is a fragile environment threatened by both natural and human activity. To reduce erosion and forest fires access to some areas is restricted. Elk are the largest animals in the park and often fairly easy to observe. Natterjack toads, common spadefoots and sand lizards are all quite common. There is an eco-tourism centre in Lesnoj, where maps, information and guided walks are on offer.

The southern two-thirds of the freshwater **Curonian Lagoon** lies in Kaliningrad, the northern third is Lithuanian water. The lagoon is a spawning ground for frogs and toads from the adjacent spit. Birds that breed, feed and rest here include white and black storks, white-tailed eagle, common crane and numerous gulls and terns. The lagoon is also a wintering area for ducks, but it can be a bleak, chilly place to explore in winter.

The Baltic coast at Svetlogorsk (JS)

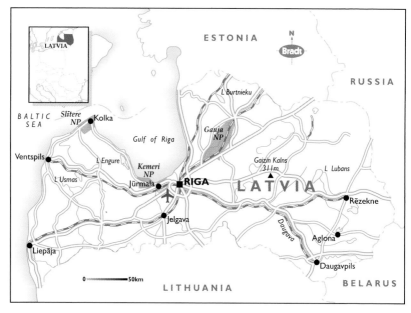

LATVIA

Latvia covers some 64,589km² and borders Estonia to the north, Lithuania to the south, Belarus to the southeast and Russia to the east. Latvia's Baltic coastline is 500km long. The population is around 2.3 million.

Stretches of Latvia's Baltic coastline are truly atmospheric. There are dunes, sandy and pebbly beaches, quiet pinewoods and headlands with isolated lighthouses that, depending upon the season, are lapped or battered by the sea. Riga Bay bites into the northern shoreline and is fringed with forests, pastures, meadows and lakes. Away from the coast Latvia is largely flat, with at the most some rolling terrain. The rural landscape is a pleasant blend of farmland, graced with low timber barns and old farmhouses, old forests and soggy bogs. The Gauja and Daugava rivers meander slowly through the heart of these habitats as they head for the Baltic. Lubans, the country's largest lake, lies in the east and together with adjacent fishponds, forms a wonderful wetland wildlife area.

Wolves are probably fairly common in Latvia, though they are not easy to see. Lynx are not quite as numerous (around 300 estimated) and brown bears are rare. The forest dormouse is also here, though it is nocturnal and difficult to observe. On the avian front an estimated 1,000 pairs of great snipe is of international significance. Some other real 'eastern' breeding species are greater spotted eagle, Terek sandpiper, citrine wagtail and parrot crossbill. Corncrake is common; in spring its rasping calls seem everywhere, whilst forests hold good numbers of grouse, owls and woodpeckers.

Latvia does not abound in reptiles, though European pond terrapins are right on the northern edge of their range here. Amphibian highlights include green and natterjack toads, the latter fairly common on the coast.

About 115 species of butterfly have been recorded, including cranberry blue and Pallas's and bog fritillaries. Latvia's wide variety of nutrient rich wetlands – bogs, mires, fens, lakes, ponds, swamps, forest ditches and channels – are all good dragonfly habitat. Several northern and southern species overlap in range.

There are three national parks, founded to preserve wildlife and their habitats and also local cultural heritage. The wetlands, meadows, pine-covered dunes and forests of **Ķemeri** are about 40km west of Riga. Beaver, red deer and elk are common and there are a few wolf and lynx to prey on them. Smaller animals include pond bat, natterjack toad and sand lizard. Marked trails and board-walks get visitors right into some swampy habitats, including Kemeri Great Bog. There is a visitor centre in Kemeri village. The northernmost point of Slitere is **Cape Kolka**, a headland complete with lighthouse, that juts into Riga Bay, 160km northwest of the capital. This is a bottleneck for migrating birds with spring best for raptors, autumn for waders. Inland, the heathland and gravel pits around Vidale are good for butterflies and dragonflies. The centrepiece of **Gauja** is a scenic valley, lined with forests, backwaters and sandstone walls along the River Gauja. Most of Latvia's typical forest animals are here. There is a visitor centre in Sigulda.

Just north of the Lithuanian border, **Pape** is a strip of land squeezed between Lake Pape and the Baltic Sea. There are dunes, beach, brackish and freshwater ponds, reedbeds and pinewoods. Pape is probably the most famous birdwatching site in Latvia, another bottleneck for birds on passage, with a bird-tower at the south of the lake, an ornithological observatory and an old lighthouse. In spring there are masses of wildfowl and seabirds, in autumn storks, raptors and songbirds. Always check the local weather before visiting.

Latvian coastline (AZ)

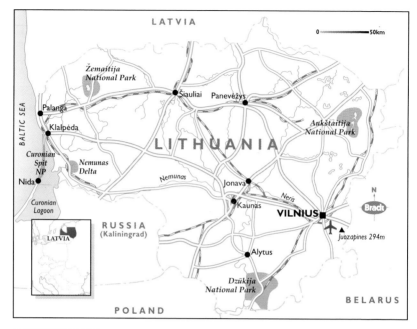

LITHUANIA

Lithuania is the southernmost of the three Baltic States. Latvia lies to the north, Belarus to the east and southeast, and Poland and Kaliningrad to the southwest. The country covers around 65,000km², with a population of 4 million. Lithuania's coastline is 99km long, 52km of which is the Curonian Spit.

Inland, Lithuania is mainly flat with some rolling country, the highest point being just 294m. Around a third of the countryside is forested, the rest either farmland or wetland. It does not take long to find a place for a squelchy walk in Lithuania; a peatbog is never far away. Bogs can be eerie places, rather bleak on the face of it, but hauntingly beautiful when their vegetation blooms in browns, reds and greens. In the southwest the River Nemunas is lined by meadows, pastures and fens and imposes itself on the landscape as it winds towards the Curonian Lagoon, where it ends in a mazy delta. Lithuania's short stretch of coast is impressive, particularly the sandy Curonian Spit, which runs into the country from Kaliningrad. The high dunes at Nida would not be out of place in Arabia.

A few hundred wolves are estimated to roam the country as well as a few lynx. Beavers are common and their dams and lodges can be found on almost every wetland. From April to August white storks are impossible to miss. There are around 13,000 pairs, the highest breeding density of the species anywhere. Two of Europe's rarest wetland birds, great snipe and aquatic warbler, breed, and winter sees a few rafts of Steller's eider just off the coast.

Just seven reptile species occur, though viviparous and sand lizards are fairly common. The 13 regular species of amphibian include common spadefoot and green and natterjack toads.

Butterflies number some 120 regular species, several at the northern edge of their range: look out for Baltic grayling. Lithuania's diverse and nutrient-rich wetlands are home to about 60 species of dragonfly, with the Nemunas Delta being one of the very best areas.

There are five national parks, founded to conserve the best of the country's natural and cultural heritage. **Dzūkija** lies on a rolling sandy plain along the Nemunas river, some 130km southwest of Vilnius. It is mostly forested and home to lynx, wolf, elk and beaver, though the two carnivores are hard to find. Birds include hazel grouse, white-tailed eagle, white-backed woodpecker and pygmy owl. A network of marked trails, board-walks and minor roads riddles the park and there are information centres in Marcinkonys and Merkine. The **Curonian Spit National Park** covers Lithuania's 50km stretch of the spit. The beaches, dunes, heathlands, meadows and pinewoods are home to a mix of reptiles, amphibians and insects and the area is a flyway for birds, mainly in autumn. There is an information centre in Smiltyne. One of the best ways to get close to wildlife at **Aukštaitija** is by canoe. Away from the water some of the old-growth forests in the north of the park have 200-year-old pines. Breeding birds include black-throated diver, black stork, lesser spotted eagle and various owls and woodpeckers. There is a visitor centre at Paluse. **Žemaitija** is another classic forested lakeland and bogland set amid rolling hills and traversed by rivers. Beavers, otters and elk are fairly common and there are some lynxes. Avoid **Lake Plateliai** in summer as it can throng with visitors. **Trakai** was established to protect the old city of Trakai, and has little wildlife interest.

The **Nemunas Delta** is a maze of channels, reedbeds, wet meadows, polders, fens, bogs and shallow lakes. There is also some farmland, forest, scrub and settlements, parts of which are inundated every spring. This is a paradise for dragonflies and birds. The delta is to the south and west of Silute on the east coast of the Curonian Lagoon. Boat-trips can be booked at an information centre in Rusne.

Out of Africa? The rolling sandy dunes at Nida. (JS)

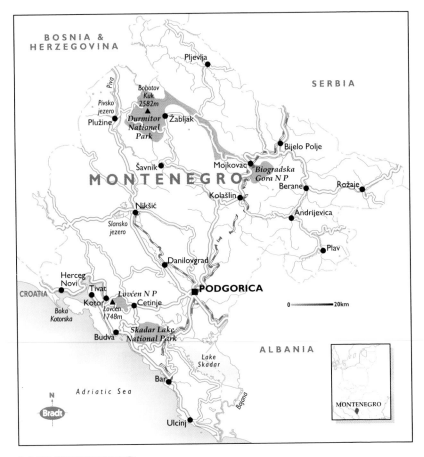

MONTENEGRO

Montenegro covers just over 14,000km² and has a population of under 640,000. Bosnia-Herzegovina lies to the northwest, Serbia to the northeast, Albania to the south, there is a short border with Croatia in the west and, in the southwest, a 293km stretch of Adriatic coast.

Montenegro may be a small country, but it is certainly not monotonous. It is possible to start the day on a sandy beach and finish on the top of a mountain, having taken in a whole range of sights and sounds on the way. The coastline is picturesque, but with far fewer tourists than most Balkan countries and dotted with maquis and salt pans where typically Mediterranean fauna can be observed. Just inland Lake Skadar is the biggest water body in the Balkans, but ultimately this is a land of mountains, some of the least visited in Europe. The locals call their country Crna Gora (Black Mountain), and this paints the right picture. The Dinaric Alps dominate the heart of the country with their jagged limestone crops and karst plateaux pocked with sinkholes and deciduous forests. In the north there are some very rugged mountains, with magnificent gorges, rapid-lined rivers, vast forests,

Lake Skadar (Skadarsko) is the largest water body on the Balkan peninsula. (LB)

alpine-like pastures and tarns, screes and numerous peaks over 2,000m. At 1,300m deep the 82km-long Tara Gorge, in the Durmitor range, is Europe's deepest (the second deepest in the world after the Grand Canyon). Forests cover almost 40% of Montenegro, with some beech, spruce, fir and black pine stands in an almost virgin state.

Brown bears, wolves and some lynx live in the more remote upland forests whilst golden jackals roam the more open lowlands. A few chamois graze at high elevations. A rich range of breeding, passage and wintering birds are found, from upland species like shore lark, snowfinch, Alpine accentor and Alpine chough, to wetland birds such as Dalmatian pelican and pygmy cormorant. Other specialities are lanner falcon and rock partridge.

This is a superb country for reptiles, with Balkan terrapin, Dalmatian algyroides, Mosor and sharp-snouted rock lizards, worm and cat snakes, Balkan whip snake and many others not uncommon. The Alpine newts in Lake Zminicko (Durmitor National Park) are often neotenous – their larvae fail to metamorphose into adults but are able to breed and reproduce young. Other specialities are Albanian pool frog and Balkan stream frog.

Butterflies include southern swallowtail, Balkan clouded yellow, Grecian and Balkan coppers, little tiger blue, blue argus and Balkan fritillary. Over 40 species of dragonfly swirl over lakes and tarns in the Durmitor range, Lake Skadar and the Ulcinjska salt pans.

There are four national parks. In the east **Biogradska** is relatively small (54km²) but has some of the Balkans' best-preserved old-growth forests, as well as glacial lakes and high peaks. There are a few brown bears, chamois, a range of bats and plenty of reptiles. In the north, **Durmitor** (390km²) includes the Tara Gorge and the country's highest peak, Bobotov Kuk (2,522m). There are brown bears, wolves and lynx, but they keep a very low profile. Chamois are easier to find. Many typical upland Balkan butterflies and dragonflies are here, too. There is an information centre near Crno jezero (Black Lake). In the southwest, close to Kotor, **Lovcén** (64km²) protects craggy limestone habitats. There are no large mammals here though there are plenty of bats and reptiles and in summer butterflies are everywhere. **Skadarsko** (Lake Skadar) is 400km² of wetlands and adjacent habitats in the south (one-third of the lake lies in Albania). This is a birdwatcher's paradise at any time of year, with plenty of amphibians, reptiles and insects to keep the all-round naturalist happy.

On the coast, in the very south, the **Ulcinjska solana** (salt pans) are an important passage and wintering site for birds. Dalmatian pelican, greater flamingo, pygmy cormorant, and various shorebirds, gulls and terns are all possible here.

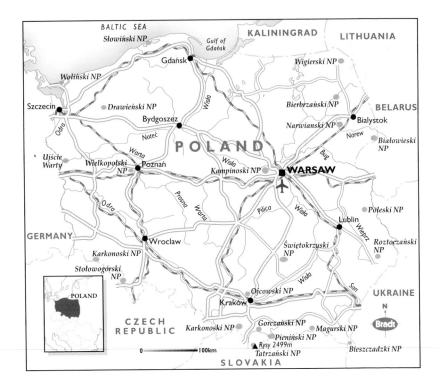

POLAND

Poland covers around 312,685km² and borders Germany to the west, the Czech Republic to the southwest, Slovakia to the south, Ukraine to the southeast, Belarus to the east and Lithuania and Kaliningrad to the northeast. In the north the Baltic coastline is 491km long. The population is around 38.5 million.

Poland is big, diverse and positively packed with places to look for wildlife. Ultimately, it is a flat country, with less than 10% of the landscape upland. The country's large plains are mainly farmed and dotted here and there with fishpond systems. Elsewhere there are forested lake districts, with over 9,000 lakes nationwide. In the northeast marshes, wet meadows and boggy forests line the routes of the Narew, Biebrza and other rivers and in the very east is Bialowieza, an old mixed forest with some huge trees. In the north the Baltic Sea and its hinterland habitats include lagoons, river estuaries, beaches, sand dunes and pinewoods. In the southeast the forested Carpathians nudge into the country before rising into the mighty Tatras, where there are alpine-like meadows, pastures, tarns, scree and rugged peaks such as Rysy (2,499m), the country's highest.

Poland is great for mammals. Beavers and elk are widespread, European bison reside in older forests and lynx, wolf and brown bear are found in the Carpathians. Alpine marmots and chamois live in the Tatras and there are colonies of spotted sousliks in the southeast. Many bats are widespread.

A wonderful mixture of coastal, wetland, woodland and mountain birds breed in Poland. Highlights include white-tailed and lesser spotted eagles, common crane, corncrake, aquatic warbler, all of Europe's woodpeckers and around 40,000 pairs of white storks: 25% of the world population.

Reptiles are not nearly as common, with probably just nine species. There are, however, 18 species of amphibian including Alpine newt, fire salamander, fire-bellied, green and natterjack toads and common spadefoot.

Poland has over 160 species of butterfly, many at the northern limit of their range. Specialities are moorland clouded yellow, cranberry blue and bog and cranberry fritillaries. In summer Poland's varied wetlands often teem with dragonflies such as green and bog hawkers, river clubtail, green snaketail and banded darter.

The hidden depths of Bialowieza Forest (R&MK)

Poland's 23 national parks protect areas of outstanding beauty, habitats and wildlife. They range from sea-level on the Baltic coastline to the highest elevations in the Tatras. The most famous is arguably **Bialowieza**, a lowland old-growth mixed forest in the east, some 220km from Warsaw. This is the best place to see wild European bison. Birds include hazel grouse, nine species of woodpecker and, in spring, flycatchers and warblers. Winter is tough here, though arguably the best season to track wolves and other large mammals. The old forest, with some magnificent limes and spruces, is littered with fungi-covered timber and swampy patches of alder. This is an atmospheric place, best visited early on a spring morning, though only with a park ranger (ask at the park HQ). **Biebrza** (150–200km northeast of Warsaw) is a maze of fens, meadows, oxbows, reedbeds, forests and traditionally worked farmland along the meandering River Biebrza and its tributaries. Beavers and elk are common and there are a few wolves. In spring and summer the region is alive with birds including lesser and greater spotted eagles, great snipe, lekking ruffs, white-winged black tern and aquatic warbler. Local maps showing colour-coded trails can be obtained at a field centre in the village of Osowiec. The **Tatra National Park** lies in the very south along the Slovakian border and embraces the country's highest mountains. There are mixed forests up to around 1,250m and dwarf pine above that. Above the treeline are typical alpine habitats, the realm of Alpine marmot and chamois. These can sometimes be accessed by ski lifts. **Bieszczady** nestles in the very southeast, by the Slovakian border. There are wild mixed forests of spruce, fir, larch and beech and sub-alpine pastures (locally called Polonina) which in summer abound in butterflies. Above all, these mountains are the Polish stronghold of large carnivores.

The **Mazurian Lake District** (200km north of Warsaw) is littered with water bodies of all sizes, mostly set in forests and with adjacent marshes. Wetland and woodland wildlife live side by side. The best period to visit is from April to September as in winter most lakes are frozen. Beaver, otter and elk are fairly common.

ROMANIA

Romania sits in the northern Balkans and covers 237,500km². It borders Bulgaria to the south, Serbia to the southwest, Hungary to the west, Ukraine to the north and northeast, and Moldova to the northeast. It also has a 225km-long Black Sea coastline in the east. The population is around 22.3 million.

Romania is large, very diverse and often wild. The mighty Carpathians dominate the heart of the country and the landscapes here are often spectacular, ranging from snow-capped peaks to picturesque rolling hills, interspersed with limestone gorges and rushing rivers. Some of Europe's wildest forests are here, including virgin stands. Transylvania is heavily forested but there are also floodplain woods, grassy basins where the fields are worked by hand and horse-drawn plough, and fishpond complexes. In the east, between the Danube and the Black Sea, is Dobrudja, a rolling plain, with dry steppe, vast crop fields, the odd oak woodland and large brackish lagoons. In the very northeast corner of the country is the Danube Delta, 4,000km² of superb wetland. Just before it enters the Black Sea the river splits into three main arms, linked by innumerable willow- and poplar-lined channels, lily-clad lakes, floating reed and rush islets, wet alder woodlands and the largest reedbeds on the continent. To the south of the delta the Black Sea coast is lined with beaches, dunes and lagoons: the very south of the coast is taken up with holiday resorts.

Romania is Europe's most important country for large carnivores, with the largest numbers of brown bears, wolves and lynx outside Russia, mostly in the upland forests of the Carpathians. Other highlights are golden jackal, marbled and steppe polecats, Alpine marmot and the near-endemic Romanian hamster.

Some real eastern bird specialities, such as Dalmatian pelican, Levant sparrowhawk, pied wheatear, paddyfield warbler and rose-coloured starling, breed in Romania. The country also has the most white pelicans (about 3,500 pairs), pygmy cormorants (over 7,000 pairs) and ferruginous ducks (perhaps 8,000 pairs) in Europe. Most winters see over 50,000 red-breasted geese on the coast.

The 20 or more species of reptile include spur-thighed tortoise, steppe runner, meadow lizard and Balkan wall lizard, whilst 17 species of amphibian include Danube crested and Carpathian newts and eastern spadefoot.

Butterflies number over 200 species. The southern Carpathians are particularly rich in butterfly habitats. Highlights are eastern and southern festoons, at least eight clouded yellow species, seven copper species, over 20 species of fritillary, Sudeten and black ringlets, Russian heath and Nogel's hairstreak, which is endemic to Dobrudja. The exact number of dragonfly species in Romania is unknown, but given the sheer number and diversity of wetland habitats, it is surely high. There are at least 30 species in the Danube Delta alone. Specialities are dark and eastern willow spreadwings, river clubtail, Balkan and sombre goldenrings.

All 11 national parks are uplands. **Retezat**, in the southern Carpathians, 390km northwest of Bucharest, is trekking country with 380km² of dense spruce, fir, larch, pine, beech and rowan forests, herb-laden meadows and pastures and dwarf pine stands. At the highest elevations there is loose scree, rugged rock walls, bleak boulder-country, isolated tarns and more than 20 summits rising above 2,000m. Mammals include Alpine marmot, chamois, brown bear, wolf and lynx. Birds include golden eagle, pygmy and Ural owls, black and hazel grouse and wallcreeper. In summer Retezat is superb for butterflies. Also in the southern Carpathians **Piatra Craiului** centres on a 25km-long steep limestone ridge: this is prime brown bear and wolf country, and another great butterfly area. The granite hills and stony steppe of **Macin** in northern Dobrudja are home to numerous reptiles, plus birds like long-legged buzzard, saker falcon, rock thrush and Isabelline wheatear. European sousliks are common and there are marbled and steppe polecats to prey on them.

The **Danube Delta** is a phenomenal wetland for wildlife. Around 82% of the delta lies in Romania (18% in the Ukraine) and is a UNESCO biosphere reserve, comprising 5,800km² including the lagoons and steppes to the south. From April to September the place buzzes with birds, amphibians and dragonflies. Mammals include wild boar, golden jackal, otter and the European mink, the latter in one of its last refuges. Though there are inhabited islands in the delta, these can only be reached by boat, and indeed the only way truly to see the delta is from the water. Boat trips run from the port of Tulcea.

The heart of the Danube Delta is only really accessible by boat. (JP)

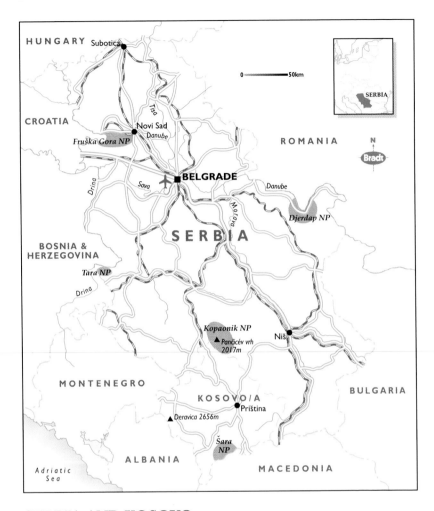

SERBIA AND KOSOVO

Serbia covers 88,361km² at the very heart of the Balkans. It has a population of around ten million and is totally landlocked, bordering Hungary to the north, Romania to the northeast, Bulgaria to the southeast, Macedonia to the south, Albania and Montenegro to the southwest, Bosnia-Herzegovina to the west and Croatia to the northwest. The southern province of Kosovo (10,908 km²; population 2.1 million) is administered by the UN and, at the time of writing, remains disputed territory: Serbia does not recognise its declared independence.

The country is roughly one-third lowland (in the north) and two-thirds montane (in the centre and south), with varied landscapes and habitats. North of Belgrade the Pannonian Plain is lowland grasslands cut through by the Danube and other rivers. Elsewhere there are rugged mountains, deep gorges, rolling wooded hills and Mediterranean-like scrub. Around 27% of Serbia is forested.

Large mammals include brown bear, wolf, golden jackal and lynx, and there are at least 28 species of bat – notably in the karst regions and river gorges. Birds include saker, red-footed falcon, eastern imperial eagle and black-headed bunting in the lowlands, and Alpine chough, nutcracker, shore lark and wallcreeper in the uplands, while all ten European woodpecker species breed. Among abundant reptiles are Hermann's tortoise, meadow lizard, Balkan wall lizard, snake-eyed skink, large whip snake and nose-horned viper. Amphibians include Balkan crested and Danube crested newts, eastern spadefoot and Balkan stream frog. Almost 200 species of butterfly occur, with eastern festoon, Balkan copper, blue argus, Freyer's purple emperor, and lattice brown amongst the many enticing species. Over 60 species of dragonfly have been recorded.

Zasavica Nature Reserve is a haven for wetland species. (KP)

The five national parks are all mountainous. **Djerdap** takes in the Miroc Mountains (southern Carpathians) and four gorges (the Iron Gates) along the Danube, where it borders Romania. Its deciduous forests, scrub and grassland are home to chamois, brown bear, golden jackal and lynx, while birds include black stork, golden and lesser spotted eagles, eagle owl and rock partridge. **Fruška Gora** is a forested hilly area that rises from the lowland of Vojvodina, 75km northwest of Belgrade. Its mosaic of broadleaved forest, steppe and farmland supports steppe polecat and European sousliks in open areas and wild boar and wildcat in the forests. Amphibians include both fire-bellied and yellow-bellied toads, while eastern imperial eagle, black woodpecker and collared flycatcher are among notable birds.

Kopaonik is 118km² of high mountain habitats. At its heart are the grasslands and mixed forests of the Suvo Rudiste plateau, while the valleys lower down are lined with rapids, waterfalls and gorges. The top predator here is the wolf, and there are plenty of birds, reptiles and butterflies. **Šara**, in Kosovo, embraces craggy alpine peaks, glacial lakes and fine forests of Macedonian pine. Mammals include chamois, lynx, wolf and brown bear, while an amazing 140 species of butterfly and over 200 species of bird have been recorded. **Tara** is a forested region along the western border with Bosnia-Herzegovina that covers parts of the Tara and Zvezda mountains, a large bend in the River Drina and the deep Drina Gorge. Its beech, fir, pine and Serbian spruce forests are said to be the country's brown bear stronghold. There are also some wolf and chamois, a dozen species of reptile and over 100 species of butterfly.

About 70km east of Belgrade, **Deliblatska Peščara** (Deliblato Sands) is a region of inland dunes, pastures, steppe, scrub and pine. The south is particularly good for birds of prey, as well as bee-eater, roller, lesser grey shrike and ortolan bunting. Reptiles abound and mammals include marbled polecat and a few wolf.

SLOVAKIA

Landlocked Slovakia covers an area of 48,845km² and is bordered to the north by Poland, to the east by Ukraine, to the south by Hungary, to the west by Austria and to the northwest by the Czech Republic. The population is approximately 5.4 million.

Slovakia is, above all, a mountainous land. There are areas of lowland floodplains, grassland and farmland in the south and southeast, mainly along the Danube and its tributaries, but ultimately it is alpine and sub-alpine mountain landscapes and habitats that dominate. The highest peak is the craggy Gerlachovsky Stit in the High Tatras (2,655m). At high elevations there are tarns, boulder country and dwarf pine stands, then forests of pine, fir, spruce and beech interspersed with pastures and meadows, dry karst regions and scenic stream valleys. Lower down still are hayfields, oak and beech woodlands, plantations, reservoirs and fish farms. Around 40% of the country is forested.

This is an important country for brown bear (800 estimated), wolf (a few hundred) and lynx (350–400). There are also Alpine marmots, a local race of chamois, and bats are widespread and often numerous. Bird highlights are montane and forest species such as hazel grouse, pygmy and Ural owls, wallcreeper and Alpine accentor. All ten European woodpeckers breed.

Slovakia is a touch too far north for several reptile species, with just ten occurring including European pond terrapin, green lizard and dice snake. Amphibians number 18 species, including fire salamander, Carpathian newt and fire-bellied and yellow-bellied toads. The Carpathian blue slug creeps around the country's uplands, too.

Over 170 species of butterfly have been recorded with species like southern festoon, lesser fiery copper and dryad on the northern edge of their ranges. Specialities include several ringlets such as large, yellow-spotted, water and Sudeten. An impressive 76 species of dragonfly occur, with wetlands along the Danube, in the west in the Zahorie region and in the east along the Latorica river being the places to explore.

The rugged peaks of the High Tatras are home to chamois and golden eagles. (MK)

This country has eight national parks, all mountainous. The **High Tatras** are home to a range of grouse, owls, woodpeckers and wallcreeper, as well as some brown bear, lynx, chamois and colonies of Alpine marmots. In summer, high flowering meadows are good for butterflies. With several peaks over 2,000m the **Low Tatras** are not low at all and have a similar fauna to the High Tatras. **Slovenský Raj** translates as 'Slovak Paradise' and it is indeed a scenic, though seriously rugged, upland area. The park's rocky ravines, plateaux and moss-and lichen-draped forests host wolf, lynx and all the forest birds that one might expect. On the Hungarian border, **Slovenský Kras** is a limestone karst region with gorges, rocky plateaux, semi-steppe grasslands and mixed forests. This is a superb area for bats, butterflies and birds of prey.

In complete contrast to the mountains, **Zahorie** is a lowland floodplain in the very west, along the Austrian border. There are wet meadows, marshes, reedbeds, pine-dotted dunes and oak, poplar and willow woodlands here, all good for amphibians, dragonflies and lowland-loving butterflies in summer. Both black and white storks are fairly common and raptors include saker falcon, red and black kites and Montagu's harrier.

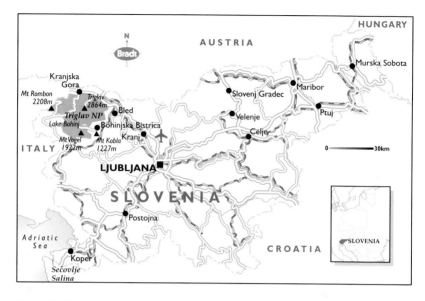

SLOVENIA

At 20,273km² Slovenia is one of Europe's smallest countries and, with just under 2 million inhabitants, one of the least populated. The country is bordered by Austria to the north, Croatia to the south and east, Italy to the west and Hungary to the northeast. There is also a short stretch of Adriatic coastline (47km) to the southwest.

Slovenia is essentially a land of mountains but, as it sits in a zone where four distinct regions meet – the Carpathian Basin, the Adriatic Sea, the Alps and the Dinaric Mountains – it has a surprising range of wildlife habitats. In the east there are farmlands, wetlands and gentle hilly country dotted with orchards and vineyards. In the south, limestone karst landscapes of gorges, sinkholes, cave systems and dry mixed forests often dominate. A brief stretch of Adriatic shore is dotted with ports, like Koper, bays, sandy and rocky beaches and salt pans. Yet, despite this, Slovenia is decidedly mountainous, with around 40% of its land area taken up by various alpine ranges, particularly the Julian Alps. Here there are many impressive and imposing snow-capped peaks of over 2,000m each with cliffs, ridges, glacial lakes, bogs, rapid-lined rivers and waterfalls, alpine pastures and meadows and vast conifer forests. Indeed, more than half the country is covered in woodland of some kind.

Brown bears have increased over the last 50 years, though a certain number can be hunted each year. The current population is between 500–700 individuals. There are perhaps a few hundred wolves and around 50 lynx. Other special mammals include Alpine marmot, chamois and Alpine ibex.

On the avian front, Slovenia is most notable for its upland and forest birds. Highlights include hazel grouse, various owls, wallcreeper, citril finch, Alpine chough and snowfinch. All European woodpeckers breed.

A good range of reptiles includes Horvath's rock lizard, Dalmatian wall lizard, Balkan whip snake and nose-horned viper. Slovenia is just about the only place in the world where the olm can be seen. Tours through the Postojna Caves pass a basin which contains a few viewable specimens.

Over 170 species of butterfly are found, including around 80 'nymphs' and several upland-dwelling ringlets such as silky, Styrian and Stygian. Dragonflies number some 70 species and Slovenia is one of the best countries to search for Balkan goldenring. Good areas include Ljubljansko barje (40 species), Lake Cerknica, the Sečovlje salt pans, peatbogs in the Julian Alps, oxbows and backwaters along the River Mura and the Goričko region (over 40 species here).

Slovenia's only national park is **Triglav**, which protects over 800km² of high mountain terrain in the Julian Alps in the very northwest of the country. At 2,864m the centrepiece is Mount Triglav, Slovenia's highest peak, which has a 3km-long and 1,000m-high rock face, the second highest wall in all the Alps. Triglav's mammals include Alpine ibex, chamois, mountain hare and Alpine marmot, and there are a few brown bears, wolves and lynx. Key birds here are ptarmigan, rock partridge, three-toed woodpecker, Alpine accentor, Alpine chough and wallcreeper. In summer this is also a great place to search for butterflies, including some localised and high-altitude species.

The **Sečovlje Salinas** are salt pans on the Adriatic coast, abutting the Croatian border. Some pans are abandoned, others still producing salt. Alongside the pans are tidal mudflats, saltmarsh, reedbeds and scrub. This is an important place for breeding, wintering and passage birds; all in all over 200 species have been recorded, 80 of which have nested. Sečovlje is also a good area for amphibians and dragonflies. There is a fee to enter this protected area, which can be explored via dyke-top paths.

Save yourself a real hike and use a chairlift to scale Triglav's peaks. (AB)

FURTHER INFORMATION

TRAVEL

Walking in Croatia: Day and Multi-day Routes. Rudolf Abraham, Cicerone, 2004. Covers walks and treks of all grades in the mountains of this scenic destination.

Latvia: the Bradt Travel Guide. Stephen Baister and Chris Patrick, Bradt Travel Guides, 2007. The most detailed English-language guide to the country.

The Julian Alp: Walking Routes and Short Treks. Justi Carey and Roy Clark, Cicerone, 2005. A guide to 60 routes of all grades of difficulty, many through good areas for wildlife.

Bosnia & Herzegovina: the Bradt Travel Guide. Tim Clancy, Bradt Travel Guides, 2007. A timely and invaluable guide for independent travellers.

Czech Republic: the Bradt Travel Guide. Mark Di Duca, Bradt Travel Guides, 2006. A lively guide to this popular country, with good coverage of national parks and wild places.

Birding in Eastern Europe. Gerard Gorman, Wildsounds, 2006. Information, site descriptions and tips on birds and birdwatching in 11 countries from the Baltic to the Black Sea.

Croatia: the Bradt Travel Guide. Piers Letcher, Bradt Travel Guides, 2007. A excellent guide for walkers and nature lovers as well as general tourists.

Slovakia: the Bradt Travel Guide. Lucy Mallows, Bradt Travel Guides, 2007. The most up-to-date guide to this small but blossoming country, including plenty of info on its mountain ranges.

Lithuania: the Bradt Travel Guide. Gordon McLachlan, Bradt Travel Guides, 2008. The most detailed English-language guide to the country.

Slovenia: the Bradt Travel Guide. Robin and Jenny McKelvie, Bradt Travel Guides, 2008. An excellent guide to this small but stunning country, including plenty of info on wild places.

Serbia: the Bradt Travel Guide. Laurence Mitchell, Bradt Travel Guides, 2007. The only English-language guide to this often neglected country, including good coverage of national parks and wildlife.

Hungary: the Bradt Travel Guide. Adrian Phillips and Jo Scotchmer, Bradt Travel Guides, 2005. A lively and colourful guide to a colourful country.

Montenegro: the Bradt Travel Guide. Annalisa Rellie, Bradt Travel Guides, 2008. The most detailed English-language guide to this 'new' destination, with good coverage of its wild places.

The Mountains of Romania. James Roberts, Cicerone, 2005. A classic guide to walking and trekking in Transylvania and the Carpathians.

Estonia: the Bradt Travel Guide. Neil Taylor, Bradt Travel Guides, 2007. Arguably the best English-language guide to the country. Packed with important background info.

NATURAL HISTORY

Field Guide to the Reptiles and Amphibians of Britain and Europe. Nicholas Arnold and Denys Ovenden, Collins, 1992. A long-standing classic for all lovers of 'herps'.

Field Guide to the Dragonflies of Britain and Europe. Klaas-Douwe B Dijkstra and Richard Lewington, British Wildlife Publishing, 2006. The definitive guide, superbly illustrated.

Whales, Dolphins and Porpoises. Mark Carwardine, Dorling Kindersley, 2002. Includes the species occuring in the Baltic, Black and Adriatic seas.

The Birds of Hungary. Gerard Gorman, Christopher Helm, 1996. The only English-language handbook to the birds of the author's adopted country.

Woodpeckers of Europe: A Study of the European Picidae. Gerard Gorman, Bruce Coleman, 2004. The definitive handbook to the European Picidae, with superb colour plates and sketches.

Collins Field Guide: Mammals of Britain and Europe. David Macdonald and Priscilla Barrett, HarperCollins, 1993. A handy illustrated guide covering every European species.

A Guide to Bats of Britain and Europe. Wilfried Schober and Eckard Grimmberger, Hamlyn, 1989. A compact but comprehensive ID guide to all European species.

Collins Bird Guide. Lars Svensson et al, HarperCollins, 2001. The best overall European bird ID book.

Butterflies of Britain and Europe. Tom Tolman and Richard Lewington, Collins, 2004. The best overall guide for the travelling lepidopterist.

WILDLIFE WEBSITES

The internet is packed with home pages related to the countries of central and eastern Europe and the wildlife found there. Some are more useful than others and only a refined search will turn up the best sites. Here are a few wildlife-related essentials and favourites:

www.blue-world.org Blue World Institute of Marine Research and Conservation. Veli Losinj, Croatia.

www.eurobutterflies.com Photos galore and ID info on Europe's butterflies.

www.herp.it Amphibians and reptiles of Europe: packed with colour photos.

www.lcie.org Large Carnivore Initiative for Europe: more on brown bear, wolf and lynx.

www.libellen.nl/europa All you need to know about Europe's dragonflies and damselflies.

www.probirder.com Background info and photos on the birds and birding sites of central and eastern Europe.

www.woodpeckersofeurope.blogspot.com ID info and photos of Europe's ten species of woodpecker.

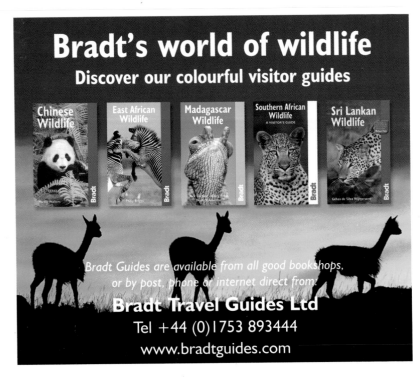